E N D O

MW00533446

Synchronicity: The Magic. The Mystery. The Meaning., *by Dr. Ken Harris, is an essential guide for understanding synchronicities, allowing you to become more aware of the value they bring to your life and the lives of others. This is a must read, written by a man who will go down in history as a gem – a great mystic, thinker and healer.*

Dr. Gilles Lamarche, Vice President of University Advancement, Life University

If you are a seeker of truth, Synchronicity: The Magic. The Mystery. The Meaning. *is a must read. In a world that appears to have lost its soul, filled with darkness, this book is like a lighthouse, shining brightly, safely showing you the way back home. Read this book, embrace its wisdom, and the benefits you'll receive will enhance your life more than you'll know.*

Dr. Bradley S. Rauch, Director, Casa Maria-Isabella Healing Center, Tepoztlan, Mexico

It's time to be awake, aware and alert to all the synchronization in life. Wow! The insights of this book are an experience that will shine a bright light into your eyes and unveil your heart to the infinite possibilities of life. I must say this book is a breath of fresh air; it speaks my language of living life in a state of gratitude and not havitude. *Remember you are never alone and are always guided from the cradle to grave and beyond. There is* no *coincidence that you stumbled across this book and that you're about to be* awakened *by this read. I encourage you to read every word, as you will be renewed. My heart is filled with joy that Ken has walked into my life at the perfect time and blessed me with the opportunity to endorse his book. It's divine!*

Dr. Roger Sahoury, international best-selling author of *Gladiators Guide to Corporate Health And Wealth;* world-renowned wellness expert; founder of Above and Beyond Holistic Wellness Centers and the SprintSet Energizing Weight Loss System

My eyes, head and heart have been opened. I have often heard the phrase "there are no coincidences" and Dr. Ken Harris's well-written and enlightening book outlines that what we think of as unexplained coincidences are actually the universe at work. We just need to be aware and watch! Harris shares stories about his own experiences with synchronicity at work and outlines how to connect to the purpose, intent and synchronicity in your own life. This book is one for the permanent library and I highly recommend this enlightening and entertaining read!

Sara Feldmann Sheehan, film producer,
www.Working-Pictures.com

Dr. Kenneth Harris's heartfelt enthusiasm for finding the synchronicities in life is contagious! The engaging personal stories he so clearly recounts in his book will inspire you to discover and learn from the synchronicities in your own life. This brilliant man weaves wisdom and truth throughout and gives the reader a sense of hope and wonderment. What a gift to the world!

Linda Roebuck, MA, visionary and founder of
A Community of Transformation, Inc.;
holistic health educator; healer

From the opening page, I was captivated. Dr. Harris opens up deeply the conversation which I believe all of us long for. He reminds us of the extraordinary quality and characteristic that we are all gifted with – connectedness. You are forever changed by his words in the most remarkable way. What a read and blessing this book is!

Dr. Jay Komarek, teacher of animal chiropractic and
producer of the documentary *Life, Adjusted*

Through short vignettes from his life experience, Ken Harris intimately shares everyday possibilities for celebrating the power of synchronicity. We remember how threads of divine resonance magically connect and guide our interlinked destinies.

Dr. Donny Epstein, developer of EpiEnergetics and author of *The 12 Stages of Healing, Healing Myths Healing Magic,* and *The Boomerang Principle*

As someone who has served others professionally in health and healing for over twenty years, I am inspired by and in awe of Ken Harris's book and his teachings. Through this book and his work, he helps people experience a re-enchantment with the world around them. Thank you, Dr. Ken.

Dr. Daniel Knowles, chiropractor and founder of Milehighchiro.org

We're just now starting to understand the magic and context of synchronicities, and Ken's book – which I was compelled to read from cover to cover in just one afternoon – offers a rare and savvy glimpse into the importance of getting out of our own way and stepping into universal flow... because that's where we can find and experience the magic that's all around us.

Lisa Najjar, psychic-medium; transformational speaker; author of *Dying to Tell You: Channeled Messages from the Famously Dead*

Our view of reality is transformed when we recognize that synchronicities are not coincidences – they are the normal course of events. The engaging personal stories in Ken Harris's book make this reality accessible to all readers.

Cornelia Wathen, MA, healer and co-founder of Holistic Health Community Inc.

In this book, Dr. Ken Harris shows us that we are never walking through life alone. Rather, guidance is constantly available from birth to death. His remarkable stories demonstrate how magical life becomes when you invite synchronicity. Not only does he inspire, he gives you the blueprint to understand the important meanings of your unique synchronicities.

Deborah Sandella, Ph.D., RN, #1 international bestselling author of *Goodbye, Hurt & Pain: 7 Simple Steps for Health, Love, and Success*

In this fascinating book, Dr. Harris weaves together a rich tapestry of stories that serve as reminders that life on Planet Earth isn't as mundane – or as random – as it may sometimes seem. These stories vividly demonstrate that we are all woven together in an interconnected, expanding, evolving web of consciousness – and spiritual awakening – that is both lawful and orderly.

Ramananda John E. Welshons, spiritual teacher and author of *One Soul, One Love, One Heart* and *Awakening from Grief*

I felt very inspired by the stories and insights in Ken Harris's book and by the basic theme of synchronicity, which is a powerful and important force in our lives. I have been guided by being aware of synchronicity for many years since reading Jung's insightful introduction to the I Ching. Ken's book is an affirmation of a very important principle in my life. Well written and moving, I recommend this book highly.

Ned Leavitt, Literary Agent,
The Ned Leavitt Agency

Dr. Ken's recollections of insight and wonder jump off of the pages and into the reader's heart! This beautiful chronicle of divine accord is a testament of how when we are living in the present, awakened, and in a state of gratitude, miracles multiply. Dr. Ken, through his memoir, demonstrates that the more we are open to see synchronicities, the more they avail us. Thank you for sharing your life through your words, your work and your boundless energetic heart!

Lorin Oneal, holistic therapist and teacher

Synchronicity is a ringing bell in consciousness, inviting the reader to examine their life for a deeper connection and meaning. Dr. Harris's stories of the ordinary and extraordinary experiences of synchronicity in his life are eye opening, instructive, and inspiring. If you're looking for more joy and synchronicity in your life, begin here!

Ken W. Stone, spiritual messenger and author of
Resonance: The Path of Spiritual Mastery

In his writings Dr. Ken Harris has captured the curiosity of nothing less than the fulfillment of one's fate, the connections we all share and the guideposts along life's path, in synchronicity. A book that grabbed my attention, as his anecdotes resonated with my own life experiences. I could not put it down and now continue to look for the connections and the meaning of these signs.

Dr. Robert DeBonis, DC, FICA, ICA
Ambassador for Chiropractic to China
and international presenter and
lecturer on chiropractic

Ken's book recounting his beautiful experiences helps the reader understand the simplicity of paying attention and "going with the flow." Ken's synchronicities will have you in awe, but the most important lesson from his book is to "Just do it!" Kudos to Ken for reminding us of how intricate and beautiful life is.

Steven A, Ross, Ph.D., President,
World Research Foundation; author; healer

SYNCHRONICITY

THE MAGIC. THE MYSTERY. THE MEANING.

DR.KENNETH HARRIS

FOREWORD BY DR. HABIB SADEGHI

The Flower of Life symbol on the cover is a visual representation of the interconnectedness of life and all beings in the universe.

SYNCHRONICITY

The Magic. The Mystery. The Meaning.

Capucia

Published by:
Capucia, LLC
211 Pauline Drive #513
York, PA 17402
www.capuciapublishing.com

ISBN: 978-1-945252-71-6
Library of Congress Control Number: 2019919782

Cover Design: Ranilo Cabo
Layout: Ranilo Cabo
Editor and Proofreader: Gwen Hoffnagle
Book Midwife: Carrie Jareed

Printed in the United States of America

Dedication

To my mentor, Dr. Bill Bahan, who woke me up
to the truth of who I am and forever changed the
course and destiny of the rest of my life.

1926 – 1983

TABLE OF CONTENTS

FOREWORD

Synchronicity happens when two things having a shared purpose or function come together at the same time in order for a particular condition or outcome to be achieved. Life has a way of using synchronicity to guide us to people who change us in fundamental ways for our personal growth and learning. That's how I felt the first time I met Dr. Ken Harris in a meeting with Dr. Norman Shealy.

As an author and lecturer in the spiritual community, I meet many lovely people who are highly self-aware and living conscious lives. Even so, it's rare to meet someone whose energy is so grounded and enduring that they draw others to them as if they had their own gravitational force about them. That's Ken, and I was no exception when it came to being drawn in by his compassionate personality and generous spirit. Perhaps it's that same energy that draws so many synchronicities to him.

His is the kind of presence that doesn't come from years of academic training, having a successful business, treating patients from around the world or any other material aspect. His natural affinity for people arises organically out of his life because he's really lived it. Anyone who meets him gets the immediate sense that he's someone who's "been there" just like them, a wounded healer who's been trained by the only real teacher in life – personal experience. That's what they relate to and what draws them in. He's the real deal.

I still feel that way when I see Ken, but I guess on a deeper level we'll always remain connected to those who change us or come along at just the right time in our lives. It's sort of like *quantum entanglement*, the term Carl Jung used to describe the theory by physicist John Bell that stated that whenever two subatomic particles interact, they never forget that association and so remain energetically entangled no matter how far apart they might be.

Ken the man, and the stories he shares here, is a constant reminder that there really is a divine plan working in harmony at a higher level that brings together people and circumstances that align with our personal energy in order to achieve a result that's for our greatest good, even if we don't understand that or can't see it at the time. Life is an exercise in letting go. If we can do that and just enjoy the ride, all those amazing entanglements can bring some pretty amazing things into our lives.

With that in mind, you're clearly not reading this book by accident. You and it found your way together so that you might learn the experience of what it means to truly surrender and simply allow your life to unfold. When we realize life isn't so complicated and we can get out of our own way, wonderful things have room to happen. I see these inspirational stories as a spiritual call to action, a beautiful invitation that welcomes all readers into a deeper understanding of what it means to trust life. It's a reminder that even you, as the observer, are being observed. No matter how dark a situation might seem, there is a greater force that's working in your favor if you know how to consciously engage it, because it's the energy we carry with us through life that always influences the context of our circumstances.

If we really are spiritual beings having temporary human experiences, then synchronicity really does exist because it's the energetic force that places people and situations along our path of personal evolution. It links us to our purpose or reason for being, and regardless of the finer details, which we call our life story, that reason for all of us is the cultivation of our consciousness.

As Ken shares some of the uncanniest experiences, you'll more than likely begin to notice synchronous experiences in your own life that you might have overlooked or written off as coincidence. It's important to revisit these experiences in order to discover what they have to teach you. I couldn't help but see parallels in my own life and even synchronicities that have occurred on a global and cultural scale.

If you take one thing from this book, let it be the invitation to let go of your white-knuckle grip on life and start cultivating the quality of acceptance that can't be acquired but only quietly realized in the peace of being. The more you can accept your circumstances as they are, the more you free yourself from them and create an energetic opening for synchronicity to lead you down a new path.

Dr. Habib Sadeghi
Founder and Director of the Bee Hive of Healing
Center, Agoura Hills, California, and
author of *The Clarity Cleanse* and
MegaZEN Well-Being Journal

PREFACE

There are more things in heaven and earth, Horatio,
than are dreamt of in your philosophy.
—William Shakespeare

I believe it is not by chance that you found your way to reading this book, and that you were somehow guided to it by unseen forces, guides or your higher self for a reason(s) not yet revealed. Perhaps it is out of mere curiosity to find personal meaning in some of your own synchronicities.

Swiss psychologist Carl Jung coined the word *synchronicity* as a way to describe a "meaningful coincidence" between two or more events in which something other than chance is involved. Synchronicities often appear to contain elements of magic, mystery and hidden meanings. Hence the name of this book came to life.

I sincerely believe there are few random coincidences in life and that the universe guides us to awaken from the illusion of separation to the reality of *Oneness*! It is my intention to give you a roadmap to help you understand why something took place in your life, the *why* or *how* of which you did not understand at that time. I hope to help you define, categorize and decipher the hidden meanings behind your synchronicities. The challenge is to first recognize them when they happen and then to try to decipher the so-called random coincidences. I believe they are happening all the time and reflect that the universe is attempting to keep you on purpose with your life's mission.

My personal synchronicities have convinced me beyond any shadow of a doubt that I have been guided throughout my entire life to meet certain people and experience certain events unfold at just the right time and place. I did not fabricate anything you are about to read. Some names are omitted to protect and respect the privacy of individuals involved, but the facts took place as described. I also include information to help you connect to your own synchronicities.

I believe we are part of a greater intelligent design, and that we have never been alone but have been guided our entire lives from beyond the physical world by some form of spiritual presence that many refer to as God. As the saying goes, "There are no coincidences – only God-incidences." I believe the universe is not random or whimsical, although it may appear to be so to our rational, logical, educated intellects, which try to convince us otherwise. Life is purposeful, and not devoid of meaning, and we are all here for a reason. It's comforting to know that we are not just flotsam and jetsam floating in the sea of life randomly bumping into each other in some haphazard, capricious way.

I've found that it's quite common for chiropractors like me, psychotherapists, and other therapeutic practitioners to find issues in their patients' lives mirrored in their own. It would appear that the student and teacher often learn a lesson together. I see everyone as my teacher, and when we meet I pay attention to what they might teach me to do or not to do. I'm certain that I alone did not consciously orchestrate or prearrange the myriad details in time and space for the stories you are about to read to have unfolded as they did.

Years ago I met legendary Yankees owner George Steinbrenner while waiting to board a plane to Tampa, Florida. Upon hearing my Yankee Stadium synchronicity story, he said, "Either what you have just shared with me is true or you simply made it up. I cannot believe anyone has that good of an imagination and could fabricate a story like yours. You cannot make this stuff up!"

I hope you find these stories to be as magical and as mystical as I do. May you be reminded of your own.

FIFTY YEARS LATER – MY YANKEE STADIUM STORY

> *There are no coincidences. We meet people intentionally who have been put on our path for a reason – sometimes sooner, sometimes later.*
> —Kenneth Harris

A few years ago, while we were vacationing on Shelter Island, my wife, Judy, and I decided to get off the island for the day to visit the main beach in East Hampton. We wanted to enjoy some body surfing in the ocean waves, which do not occur at Shelter Island.

When we left the ferry in Sag Harbor, I made a wrong turn and took the road that takes you into the town of

Amagansett, a couple of miles from East Hampton. If you are familiar with the Hamptons, you know that during the summer months there is so much traffic it can take a very long time to go just a couple of miles, so we decided to stay at the Amagansett Beach area and forgo trying to drive to the East Hampton beach.

Being professional beachgoers, we loaded up our "wonder wheel cart" with all our gear and proceeded to set up "Camp Harris" with our two beach chairs, two umbrellas, two blankets, towels, table and cooler all perfectly in place with a bird's eye view of the ocean. It was early morning and there were very few others present so we had the perfect spot of our choosing.

About half an hour later, a gentleman walking with a cane came down to the beach with a small towel and proceeded to sit right in front of us, somewhat obscuring our much-valued and appreciated ocean view. My first impulse was to ask him to please find another place to sit since the beach was practically empty, but I supposed from the way he had navigated with his cane that he might have recently had hip surgery and could not go any farther. He struggled to sit down on the small towel, and with his back to us stared out at the ocean and watched the constant flow of waves on the shoreline just as we were doing. After a short time, he attempted to get himself back up off the towel using his cane, but with great difficulty. I politely offered to help him get on his feet but he refused, saying his doctor told him he needed to learn to do this for himself.

I told him that I knew he must have had hip replacement surgery, which takes time to heal, and that he shouldn't put too much weight on a newly replaced hip. He asked how I knew so much, and I replied that I was a chiropractor and had seen hip-joint patients walk the way he had when he first entered the beach area.

When he finally stood up, he put on a New York Yankees baseball cap. A voice inside of me – the voice of intuition – said, *Ken, be kind and tell him about your Yankee Stadium experience and make his day.*

Here's a recap of the story I shared with him: When I was fourteen years old, I lived in the South Bronx and played on a baseball team that won the citywide championship tournament. The league we played in was the precursor to the now famous Little League. Back then we were known as the Little Fellers League. As a reward for winning the championship, we were given the opportunity to play a three-inning exhibition game at Yankee Stadium before a regularly scheduled night game between the New York Yankees and the Kansas City Athletics. I had the opportunity to see all my baseball heroes, sitting in the dugout with the likes of Mickey Mantle, Yogi Berra, Whitey Ford, Billy Martin, etc. A dream come true for a fourteen-year-old. My claim to fame that fateful night was when I got up to bat and hit a home run to right center field about two hundred and fifty feet over a temporary fence that had been installed just for our exhibition game. My fifteen seconds of fame had just taken place at the ripe young age of fourteen!

Unfortunately back in 1960 we did not have cell phones or portable video cameras to capture the moment. As a matter of fact, my own mother, who was a devoutly religious person, had to swear on the bible to my children that it did in fact happen!

Back to the man on the beach. When I finished telling my story, he asked me two questions: Where did I move to after leaving the Bronx, and what high school did I attend? I told him I had moved to Astoria, Queens, and had attended Long Island City High School. He looked at me and said, "You're Kenny Harris and I'm Richie Kosick and I know what you just told me is true because you and I played on the same baseball team!"

I could not believe what I had heard him say! I remotely remembered his name, although I could not for the life of me recognize his appearance. He told me that although he, too, had not recognized me by my appearance, he would never forget the story of my hitting a home run at Yankee Stadium.

I was wearing only my bathing suit and he had identified me accurately from the story alone. To say I was elated would be an understatement, and I promptly called Judy over to meet my old teammate! I told Richie I had been going to ask him to move when he first sat down, and he said he was glad that I refrained because if I had he doubted if he would have spoken to me at all afterward. Thank God I listened to my intuition and did not ask him to move over.

He told me that for some unknown reason he felt compelled to visit Amagansett Beach that day, and that he, like us, used to rent a house in Amagansett and visit with his family during the summer months. He said he was on his way to Montauk but was innately directed to stop by the old beach at Amagansett for one more nostalgic visit! Fate had me take a wrong turn off the ferry, and at the same time urged Richie to stop on his way out to Montauk so we could reconnect after fifty-plus years!

Richie told me that he lived in Brooklyn but that Nick Calderone, our former pitcher, lived somewhere in New Jersey. I asked him if he had a phone number for Nick and he said yes, so we called him from the beach that very moment. After speaking briefly with Nick, I discovered that we live one town away in northern New Jersey. We agreed to meet the following week at a local diner. I told him I would be wearing a Yankees baseball cap so he would know who I was.

As planned, the following Friday I drove the short distance from my town to his to meet for breakfast. I parked my car and walked a short distance up the hill towards the restaurant, and saw someone standing outside the door to the diner looking at his phone. He looked up and motioned for me to come over to him. I said, "Hi Nick! So happy to see you again after fifty-four years." He nodded in agreement and we spoke about my meeting Richie on the beach the previous week. We talked about setting up a reunion with some of the remaining team members and our former coach, who was still alive at age eighty-seven and living in Manhattan. I then asked him to join me for breakfast as we planned, and he said he had already eaten but that he would set up a reunion dinner and call me with details. I asked him if we could take one photo to show our wives what we looked like together. He agreed and a passerby took a photo of the two of us. He then said goodbye and walked away in search of his car.

At the time I thought it was strange that he had eaten breakfast before I arrived, but I just wrote it off as rudeness and let it go at that. You cannot imagine my surprise when about twenty minutes later, while I was taking my usual morning walk in a nearby park, I got a cell phone call from someone claiming to be Nick Calderone, wanting to know if I was intending to keep our breakfast date. I said, "Nick, do you not remember that we just met outside the diner and had a conversation and even took a photo together?" The caller said, "That was you? I walked right by the two of you but didn't see your Yankee cap, and it looked like you knew each other. I'm inside the restaurant waiting to meet you now!" I immediately got back into my car, drove to the diner, went inside and met with the real Nick Calderone! Who the other gentleman was will remain a mystery to me, and why he pretended to be Nick will remain an unanswered question.

Some months later seven members of the team got together for a reunion dinner with our old baseball team coach. It was a heartfelt time. Richie had an old newspaper clipping showing a photo of our team with me, him and Nick standing alongside one another. I finally had proof positive to show my kids that I played baseball as a teenager and was telling the truth. I was vindicated at last!

A CALL TO THE MOUNTAIN

*Once you make a decision,
the universe conspires to make it happen.*
—*Ralph Waldo Emerson*

In June of 2007 I traveled to Peru, spending seventeen days in the Sacred Valley, which included a trip to the world-famous Machu Picchu. I had the opportunity to spend both a sunset and a sunrise experience in this most magical place, along with some sixteen other spiritual pilgrims on my tour. How this all came about is another example of how the universal mind operates.

I had stayed up late one night, which was very unusual for me. I find myself going to bed early and rising early on most days year round. I enjoy the quiet and solitude that the early morning hours provide. That night I turned on the TV and watched a documentary about the Valley of the Sun narrated by the actor Leonard Nimoy, AKA Mr. Spock, of *Star Trek* fame. It was all about the lost city of Machu Picchu and the various legends surrounding its history, use and purpose. I was completely enthralled by this documentary and profoundly felt a calling to visit this place to experience it firsthand.

The next morning when Judy woke up, I shared my deep desire to visit this place, telling her the details of the documentary. She asked me one question: "How high is the mountain?" She suffers from altitude sickness, and when I informed her that it was quite high – somewhere between eight and eleven thousand feet above sea level – she said she understood why I wanted to go but that I would be going alone without the pleasure of her company. I told her I did not know when or how I would go, but when the time was right I would find my way to Peru and Machu Picchu.

Well, the universe was listening. When I went into my study to check my email for the day, I discovered, much to my delight and surprise, an email from someone I had met some seven years prior in Boulder, Colorado, at an energy healing conference. Dr. Deb Sandella, a psychotherapist and transformational healer, said she was organizing a group to travel to Peru and Machu Picchu the following June and did I want to go? Needless to say, I immediately called Deb to register.

This is just another example of how stating one's intention can bring about its manifestation – effortlessly.

The trip to Peru and the Sacred Valley was one I will never forget. I climbed the second peak behind Machu Picchu, called Huayna Picchu, on Father's Day, along with four other members of our group of sixteen and three Peruvian guides. It was not without great physical effort on my part to ascend this peak, some 3,500 feet above the ancient city of Machu Picchu, making it about 11,000-plus feet above sea level. It was one of the hardest climbs I had ever attempted in terms of steepness of grade and rarity of atmosphere. At age sixty-one it was definitely a challenge for me, but I knew I would probably never get another opportunity to visit this place, so as they say – I went for it! I was glad I did. It was a spectacular view of a lifetime to see the surrounding mountains and Machu Picchu below us in the distance. It appeared as if we were in an airplane looking down upon the terrain below. Add to all this the special moment when the seven of us who had made it to the top stood in a circle atop this mountain while I read an original poem I had written in 2001 about the World Trade Center tragedy, to honor the memory of all those who perished on that fateful day:

Out of the Ashes
Call me by my true name
My true name is – I am
Forms come
Forms go
I remain

Ashes to ashes
Dust to dust
From before birth to after death
I remain

There was never a time when I was not
Oh, death where is thy sting!
Heaven holds all of us in eternity!!!

MEETING RAM DASS,
AKA DR. RICHARD ALPERT

We're all just walking each other home.
—Ram Dass

They say the Hawaiian island of Maui has some magic and mystery all its own. I suppose that's why some very prominent people choose to live there at least part of the year. One well-known spiritual teacher, Ram Dass (formally known as Dr. Richard Alpert), has lived there since a stroke left him partially paralyzed and unable to travel.

Growing up in the 1960s, I was very aware of Ram Dass and his teachings. As a Harvard professor with a Ph.D. in clinical psychology, he teamed up with colleague Timothy Leary to experiment on campus with the psychoactive drug LSD and promoted its use by students. They were both eventually fired.

Ram Dass then traveled to Mexico and India, and after a series of seemingly unrelated events found his way to the ashram of Neem Karoli Baba, a guru with a large following, many of whom were westerners. He was forever changed by his time at the ashram. He returned to the US and wrote the best-selling book *Be Here Now*, and is forever to be identified as a leader of the new age mystical movement of consciousness-expanding practices.

While on vacation in Maui visiting my friend Wayne Dyer, I got the innate feeling that I was supposed to meet Ram Dass, but at the time did not know why. I called my friend John Welshons in New Jersey and asked him how I might be able to connect with Ram Dass. John is a well-known meditation teacher and author, and if anyone knew how to get to see Ram Dass, it would be him. He told me it was very rare for Ram Dass to see anyone for one-on-one visits, but he gave me his private number, gave me permission to use his name and wished me luck.

I immediately called and left a message for Ram Dass. I waited several days but no answer came back. I called John and he suggested I try to leave one more message. I took his advice, hoping it just might work the second time around. Several more days passed, but still no response.

As I was preparing to return home to New Jersey, I received a text message that my flight had been canceled and I needed to reschedule. As I was about to call and reschedule my flight, feeling somewhat annoyed about the cancellation, my phone rang and it was Ram Dass's secretary inviting me to come for a visit with him the next day! I smiled to myself about the synchronicity in that flight being cancelled, opening the way to meet Ram Dass.

Early the next morning I awoke and prepared for the hour-long drive across the island to Ram Dass's home. After my usual morning meditation and yoga routine, I began to think about what I could take to him as a gift. The image of flowers came to me, and I remembered a friend and fellow chiropractor telling me that she had a friend who was an excellent florist in Maui and if I ever needed some flowers to simply call her. I gave her a call and she met me on the highway en route to Haiku with a bouquet to present to Ram Dass.

As I was driving, I wondered what I would say or ask once I arrived there. At the time nothing clearly came to mind. I just knew I was supposed to meet with him and trusted that Spirit would direct me at the right time and in just the right way.

When I arrived at his secluded home facing the ocean at the end of a long road – a beautiful and idyllic setting – I was cordially greeted by his secretary, who took my flowers and put them in a vase with water saying I could give them to Ram Dass myself. My experience upon first entering his study was one of profound peace. I could feel his calm presence many feet before reaching my seat in front of him.

It felt as if time was being suspended and I instantly knew that I was in the presence of someone special. My body relaxed and my breathing was deep and calm. Due to a stroke he had suffered several years earlier that left him partially paralyzed, he was sitting in a wheelchair. I distinctly remember making eye contact with him and how a profound feeling of love flowed between the two of us even before a single word was uttered.

He began by asking me what had brought me there on that day. I said I had an innate feeling that he and I were supposed to meet for some unknown reason. In the stillness of the moment, my late friend Shyamdas came to mind and I could sense his presence in the room. Shyamdas was a well-known Vedic scholar and Bhakti Yoga musician I had met several years earlier in Costa Rica at the Blue Spirit Retreat Center, which was founded by Stephan Rechtschaffen of the Omega Institute in Rhinebeck, New York. I knew from my friendship with Shyamdas that he and Stephan made yearly visits to Maui to visit with Ram Dass, who was connected to Omega and even had a memorial library built there in his honor.

What I did not realize before my visit was that I was still processing some unresolved grief over Shyamdas's sudden, untimely death in a traumatic motorcycle accident while in India where he lived part of the year. I began to tear up and felt some deep grief come upon me in Ram Dass's presence. He looked at me, touched his hand to his third eye (in the center of the forehead) and motioned upward towards the sky. He said, "Ken, Shyamdas is now with Krishna" (another word for God in the Hindu religion). At hearing his words, I felt an immediate sense of peace come over me around the sudden passing of my dear friend.

In retrospect, it's no surprise to me now why I felt the compulsion to visit with Ram Dass. Shyamdas used Ram Dass to communicate to me that he was fine, that I could rest knowing he was with the Source of creation, and that I could move on.

I shared with Ram Dass that Shyamdas was like a brother to me and that I believed him to be part of my spiritual family. I used the Yiddish word *mishpucha* to explain how I felt about Shyamdas. *Mishpucha* means a member of one's tribe or family. Much to my surprise, Ram Dass started heartily laughing, and when he finally composed himself said, "Ken, I know what *mishpucha* means! I'm Jewish!"

I felt somewhat embarrassed, having forgotten that he had come from an upper-class, privileged Jewish family, but in a matter of seconds I went from crying about the loss of my friend, to embarrassment, to laughter!

After the laughter subsided, he then asked me several questions ranging from my interest in spiritual practices to how I came to know both John Welshons and Wayne Dyer. I told him I had met John several years earlier at one of his meditation retreats in New Jersey and that I had been treating Wayne for some health concerns after having synchronistically met him walking outside his condo in Maui the year before. Like Shyamdas, I believed Wayne was my *mishpucha* as well.

As I said goodbye I stood up and leaned closer to him to say, "Thank you for meeting me today. You have blessed me more than you could ever know." He grabbed me with his one functional arm and with tears in his eyes said, "Ken, it is you who have blessed me today by your visit." I will never forget the look of gratitude and love that radiated from him on that special day.

I honestly don't remember driving back across the island. It felt like I was in an altered state of consciousness, which lasted several days after the visit and exchange with him. I believe our meeting was divinely arranged by Spirit to assuage my grief around the loss of my dear friend Shyamdas.

Annoyance at an airline cancellation had turned into a rare and amazing experience. A good lesson to remember: sometimes an unexpected change of plans can turn out to be a blessing in disguise!

HARRIS, HARRIS, EVERYWHERE I GO!

We are like islands in the sea, separate on the surface but connected in the deep.
—Thomas Moore

On New Year's Day, as part of our family tradition, Judy and I drive up to the Mohonk Mountain House in New Paltz, New York, to say some prayers and set our intentions for the coming year, sometimes with friends but often it's just us.

This year several friends accompanied us on our hike to Skytop Tower, at the highest point on the mountain, from which you can see six surrounding states – a spiritual vista point, metaphysically speaking. It was somewhat windy, so we decided to hold our meditation circle back at the Mountain House, where we looked for a quiet place away from people and activity left over from the New Year's celebration the night before. In the past we had used a room on the first floor near the west dining room but unfortunately it was not available to us. I went upstairs to the parlor room but that, too, was occupied.

I then remembered that some years before we had used a room on the third floor overlooking the lake. I climbed up to the third floor and, much to my surprise, saw a sign in front of the room that read "Harris Family Gathering." I felt a little giddy at the thought of finding some possibly related Harris family members sitting there waiting to greet me. But the room was completely empty, with chairs set up in a circle just waiting for us to sit down in total peace and quiet so we could begin our group meditation!

And this was the second time within six months that I had run into a "Harris Family Gathering"! While vacationing on Shelter Island at the Ram's Head Inn, which has a small private beach, I started a conversation with a fellow guest who, along with his brother, was wearing a Duke University baseball cap. I asked them if they were Duke wannabees or had actually graduated from Duke. One gentleman replied that yes, both he and his brother, Dr. Harris, were fellow Duke graduates! I introduced myself as Dr. Harris also, and discovered that his brother was a medical doctor from Huntington, Long Island, and that we knew many people in common. His entire family was there for a family reunion. No relation to me, but it was nevertheless fun to meet people who shared my namesake.

Several years ago while on a retreat in the Costa Rican rainforest, I met another Dr. Ken Harris, from Pennsylvania. He was a radiologist and we were in the same retreat class on mindfulness-based meditation training.

But the most bizarre encounter with another Ken Harris happened many years prior right in my own office when a patient filled out the new patient form and wrote – what I thought was a mistake – my name in the space for the patient name. When I started to give the case history form back to him, I also noticed that his date of birth was identical to my own! I said to him that there must be some misunderstanding on his part, at which point he took out his driver's license and showed it to me. We had the same name and we were born on the same day and year! Go figure! What does all this synchronicity mean? I'm not sure, but it always brings a smile to my face when I meet another Harris!

THE STEPPINGSTONES TO
FRIENDSHIP

While I was vacationing on Maui, a pop-up on my computer screen advertised a fundraiser for a movie called *Love Bomb*. I clicked on the link out of pure curiosity – I had never seen the words *love* and *bomb* in the same sentence. The movie was about the travels of three young, recently graduated chiropractors on a mission trip in Peru. It showed them traveling from village to village all over the country, adjusting hundreds of grammar-school-aged children. I was emotionally moved after watching the movie trailer and decided to support this project as an associate producer of the film.

Over a period of several months I had several conversations with the project writer-producer and director, Dr. Rhea Zimmerman, who fell in love with and eventually married one of the other volunteers, Dr. Austin Komarek. I was fortunate to be invited to their wedding held at Dr. Zimmerman's home in northern California.

At the wedding, which was one of the most beautiful I had ever attended, I had the good fortune to meet the groom's dad, Dr. Jay Komarek. He is somewhat of an icon in my profession, well known as "the horse chiropractor." Our encounter, albeit brief, left me hoping I would get to know him better down the road as a friend and colleague.

Then, while attending another seminar, I ran into Dr. Jay again when he received an award as Chiropractor of the Year at the Mile-High Chiro event in Denver. I took the opportunity to reconnect with him there and our friendship has deepened and grown since then. We are now, along with several others, founding members of the Chiropractic Elder Wisdom Council, hoping to give back our combined 200-plus years of experience to the young generation of new chiropractors.

In retrospect, I did not know at the time that by supporting a film I would get to meet and connect with someone like Dr. Jay simply by being invited to attend his son's wedding. Life has a funny way of connecting people through seemingly unrelated events. We just never know why we are compelled to do certain things like support a film or attend a wedding or seminar to find someone with whom to create and share a project that will outlive both of us and become part of our combined legacies!

PRAYERS ANSWERED!

> *There will always be a reason why you meet people.*
> *Either you need them to change your life or you're the*
> *one that will change theirs.*
> —Madeline Sheehan

While in Florida trying to escape the cold, snow and ice of the northeast, Judy and I enjoy walking the beach at the Barefoot Beach Preserve in Bonita Springs. We love the sound and smell of the Gulf waters, which help set the tone for the rest of our day, much like a meditation experience.

On one morning walk, we noticed that as a result of an overnight thunderstorm millions of shells had washed ashore as well as millions of dead fish killed by a red tide common to the Gulf waters in winter. We were both engaged in picking up some shells to take back to our grandchildren in New Jersey, especially for our granddaughter Avery who is quite the artist and loves to paint seashells. Judy was ahead of me by at least twenty feet. As I bent down to pick up a shell, a woman bent down next to me, also picking up some shells. Somehow we started a conversation and I asked her a question about one of the shell casings I had found, not recognizing what it once housed.

As we continued to speak it became evident that she was quite knowledgeable about the beach life forms we were collecting there together. So I asked her if she lived in Bonita. She said no, but she did live on Long Beach Island in New Jersey. I said I, too, lived in New Jersey, but not on the beach. I told her that I lived in Waldwick in Bergen County and that I had many patients who owned summer homes on LBI.

We continued to walk and talk, picking up seashells. As I was about to walk ahead and join Judy, who was just ahead, for some unknown reason I started to share more with her. I asked if she had heard that based on the Hubble telescope discoveries, scientists maintain that there are more stars in the Milky Way galaxy than there are grains of sand on every beach on our entire Earth. She remarked that she had heard that fact as well. I then told her that according to scientists there are more atoms in one grain of sand than there are stars in the galaxy. She said she was not aware of that fact. I then told her that there are potentially more antibody-antigen formations in the human body than there are stars in the Milky Way.

She looked at me with great surprise and asked, "You mentioned that you are a doctor and have patients who own homes on LBI, yes? So what kind of a doctor are you?" I replied that I am a vitalistic chiropractor. She had a look on her face as if to say *I knew it! You must be a chiropractor!* She promptly informed me that her husband, her son and her dad were all chiropractors! I later came to discover that her husband had been a former student of mine, and that on this day she had been praying to her recently deceased father asking for some help with a personal challenge she was facing and working on emotionally.

She teared up and said, "I think my dad sent me here today to this beach to meet you, and that my prayers will be answered by having met you, Ken." She had had a great deal of company visiting the entire week but that day felt the need to be alone and reflect and had decided to drive from Ft. Myers Beach to Barefoot Beach for a quiet walk in solitude.

I'm glad I spoke up and asked some questions, and even more thankful I decided to share some tidbits of information regarding stars, grains of sand and antibodies! Who knew how fast things can change – in a moment!

We joined Judy and they shared childhood stories of growing up in a chiropractic family and all the challenges of being different from the other kids at school, like being the only ones who received adjustments instead of taking medication when ill.

I truly believe this woman's deceased father had something to do with our meeting that fateful day on Barefoot Beach. This is an example of what we might label *precursor synchronicity*. Her dad encouraged her in a dream state the night before to seek an answer on a beach that was over half an hour away from the one right outside her condo. After engaging in a brief conversation, we discovered the connections: her husband was a former student of mine; her father and Judy's father were both chiropractors; her son needed some guidance; and I was more than happy to provide mentorship should he be interested. I later met with him at my office, as well as on Long Beach Island where he lived and practiced. Prayers answered for sure!

From the time we met Diane on the beach in Bonita Springs, I put anniversary posts on Facebook recounting the story of our synchronistic encounter on that fateful day. We had become Facebook friends, so my posts showed up on her friends' feeds as well.

Exactly one year later...

Judy and I decided to try a new beach walk in Naples, Florida, about a half-hour drive from the Barefoot Beach Preserve where we originally met Diane. Again, there had been a storm the night before, washing up millions of seashells just as it had in Bonita one year before – another opportunity to get some rare and unusual seashells for the grandkids to paint as gifts for us. Well, don't you just know, another woman came alongside me and we also started a conversation about the seashells we were finding. I picked up the same type of unusual sea casing I had found with Diane, only this time I knew its name and told her the story about meeting Diane.

She stood up (we were both bending over) with a look of complete amazement on her face and exclaimed, "You must be Ken Harris!" I said, "Yes, I am. How do you know me?" She said she had seen the story on Facebook about fifteen minutes prior and had just gotten off a phone call with her friend, Diane. They had been discussing the story before she had left for her beach walk, as Diane had reposted it herself earlier that morning on her own feed line. My new friend, Mary, and Diane were best friends, and both had homes on LBI.

Go figure! What are the mathematical chances of meeting two women, one year apart, picking up seashells on two different beaches, who happened to be best friends for years and lived on the same island and were speaking to each other minutes before about me and the beach encounter one year prior? I am no mathematician, but I would have to say the odds are quite slim to none.

We immediately called Diane from the beach, knowing that what all three of us had experienced was no chance encounter! We understood that Diane, Mary and Ken were destined to meet, and that some unknown force arranged all the myriad details for the encounter to take place. Coincidence, chance or randomness operating here? I'll let you decide!

PREMONITION – JOHN DENVER'S PLANE

> *Until you make the unconscious conscious,*
> *it will direct your life and you will call it fate.*
> —C. G. Jung

In April of 1989, while vacationing with my family at a Scottsdale, Arizona, resort, Judy asked if we could take a short drive to Carefree, Arizona, to have lunch at another resort. I agreed, and along with my daughter, Alexa, and son, Ryan, we drove to Carefree.

While waiting to be seated, I noticed that one of the men in front of us looked like the famous singer John Denver. I was a big fan and wanted an opportunity to speak with him should one arise. When the hostess returned to seat my family, I asked her if we could please sit close to his table. She happily agreed and sat us quite near him, his then-pregnant new wife and an English gentleman. I overheard them speaking about a new aircraft he was about to purchase.

When the opportunity opened, I began a lovely exchange that lasted about twenty minutes. I told him how much I appreciated his work and that I had all his albums and used many of his songs in my workshop presentations. I'd also sent him an invitation, some years prior, to be a keynote speaker at one of the Whole Health Institute gatherings we held each year in Estes Park, Colorado. His schedule unfortunately hadn't permitted him to attend, but he did remember the invite.

Before John left the restaurant, he came over to our table to thank us for the conversation and stuck out his hand to shake mine. As he held my hand a very strange event occurred for me. I got an intuitive flash that he was going to die in a plane crash! I'd never had such an experience before, so it was quite unsettling.

After he left, I shared my vision with Judy, Alexa and Ryan, but they didn't seem to take it seriously. I was quite upset and had wanted to tell him not to buy that plane they were discussing over lunch.

We returned to our hotel and my family went swimming; the children splashed in the smaller pool and Judy and I dipped our toes in the larger, adult pool. Within twenty minutes the children ran over, telling me the radio was broadcasting news that there'd been an accident when Mr. Denver's plane had taken off from the Carefree airport. His plane apparently hit another plane, causing his to flip over. It was a miracle that no one was seriously injured.

As we all know, John died in a plane crash in Monterey Bay, California, eight years later. I happened to be watching TV when the news reported his death, and burst into tears over the loss of a man I considered my friend and inspiration!

Should I have told him of my premonition? Would it have changed his mind regarding buying that plane? I will never know.

Our entrance and exit on this plane of existence, in my opinion, is set in stone the day we incarnate. I suspect that John, like the rest of us, had an appointed time to depart this realm and that my sharing my premonition with him would *not* have altered his plans to fly planes and soar in the sky, even though he might be soaring in the sky to this day. I believe this is called "destiny."

GO SEE DONNY EPSTEIN!

I trust everything happens for a reason.
—Oprah Winfrey

Some years ago I'd been going through a period of extreme emotional distress that manifested in constant neck, shoulder and arm pain. I had a pinched nerve. I'd been getting temporary relief from my local chiropractic colleagues, but it didn't last. Anyone who's suffered from chronic pain knows how debilitating it can become. At the time I was renting a summer cottage at the Mohonk Mountain House in New Paltz, New York. I'd been introduced to this magical place in 1970 when I attended the wedding of my best friend, Dr. Bob Rabin.

I vividly remember my introduction to Mohonk Lake and this historic landmark hotel. It was a complete déjà vu – a profound, visceral feeling of inner knowing that I'd been there before. When I gazed upon the rock formations around the lake, it truly felt as if I knew it, so much so that I was overwhelmed with emotion and could not speak. Judy was standing alongside me and, noticing my silence, asked me, "Ken, are you okay?" I composed myself and replied, "I've been here before." Judy said, "Not with me, you haven't," to which I immediately replied, "Not in this lifetime."

I was in intense pain and needed relief. I had a vivid dream in which I was instructed to seek help from Dr. Donny Epstein. I remember wondering how I was going to contact him, as I hadn't seen or spoken to him in decades. I knew that he lived somewhere in Colorado. Was I being told to get on an airplane and fly to Colorado to seek him out?

Back in 1974 I was an instructor at the Columbia Institute of Chiropractic and Donny was one of my students. He would always sit up front and would often come up after class to ask me some very significant, thought-provoking questions, as he was a serious and very bright student.

After graduating, he went on to create and develop the popular chiropractic healing system known as Network Spinal Analysis. He has taught this system all over the world to thousands of doctors and has become an icon in the chiropractic profession.

I was opening my mail the morning after having my vivid dream and was immediately drawn to open a catalog from the Omega Institute. Much to my delight I discovered that Donny was offering a workshop there that very same day entitled The Twelve Stages of Healing, based on his newly released book of the same title.

I interpreted this "coincidence" as a sign from Spirit that I should go over to Omega to seek his help with my ongoing pain. I told Judy that I was planning to drive forty-five minutes from Lake Mohonk to the Omega Institute in Rhinebeck, New York. When I arrived, I checked in and walked to the pavilion where the class was being held. Donny was sitting by himself next to the adjusting table. All the other participants were nowhere to be seen, as minutes before I arrived they'd been dismissed to go to lunch.

Donny greeted me by name with a big hello, a good sign that he remembered me as his former instructor. He asked me how he could be of service and I told him of my ongoing physical challenges and that I'd dreamt of him the night before and was *told* to visit him for help.

Donny had me sit down on the adjusting table – not lie down, which is the standard when receiving chiropractic adjustment. I thought this was unusual and wondered how he was going to adjust me. He then proceeded to walk around the table in a circle several times in complete silence. Suddenly, without warning or words, he got behind me and did a light thrust adjustment to my neck. What happened next was magical! Without warning my arms lifted into the air in a wave-like motion and the pain immediately left me for the first time in months! I had never (and never since) received this type of adjustment from anyone.

B. J. Palmer, who was known as the developer of chiropractic, once said that one chiropractor will get better results than another because "when the chiropractor's innate giving in the adjustment is able to contact or commune with the patient's innate receiving of the adjustment, the results will be better than expected." He's also credited with saying, "When an adjustment is given at the right time, place and direction, results are guaranteed to follow."

What I experienced that day with Donny was nothing short of miraculous for me. It's no coincidence that I dreamt of him and he just happened to be teaching nearby and the Omega catalog arrived the next morning and when I opened it, it was at the exact page describing the information about his workshop.

Pay attention to the universe. I believe it's constantly guiding us with signs from beyond. I followed the trail and was gifted with immense pain relief and joy.

A Series of Unexpected Encounters

Ever since that day in 1970 when Judy and I first went to Mohonk Mountain House we have enjoyed hikes there in the fall, cross-country skiing in winter and swimming in the lake during the summer months. We rented a summer cottage there for over twenty-five years, and I commuted over an hour from my chiropractic office in northern New Jersey so that my children could have fond memories of summers on the mountain.

During those years I had the opportunity to befriend and treat many members of the Smiley family which had founded Mohonk Mountain House. They were of Quaker heritage and gravitated to all things natural, including in regard to healthcare. Their keen interest in preserving the land around the hotel for future generations resulted in the Mohonk Preserve. Four US presidents visited Mohonk and several movies have been filmed there. Every day for the last 150 years, come rain or shine, tea and cookies have been served in the lake lounge and porch areas starting at 4pm and ending promptly at 5pm. No matter how quiet the hotel seems to be, people miraculously appear in droves to gobble up the homemade cookies and Mohonk house blend tea. Our twenty-fifth wedding anniversary, as well as my fiftieth birthday celebration, took place there, and I've hosted several international health conferences alongside the beautiful lake. Judy and I love this place so much that we've instructed our children to spread our ashes there when we leave this earth school for the great beyond.

One afternoon I showed up to get my tea and cookies and find a seat on the porch overlooking the lake. A man sat down beside me and we engaged in some casual conversation. He shared that he was a minister attending a religious conference with his wife, who is also a minister. They each had their own churches, his on one side of Mohonk Mountain and hers on the other side in High Falls. We discussed our mutual love of the nature around the grounds and I explained how I had found Mohonk when attending my friend's wedding so many years prior.

I asked him how he became a minister, to which he responded that he'd been a successful businessman who got sick with cancer and was not given long to live, but then he had a religious experience in a conversation with a pastor and became healed as a result. He said, "I got Jesus out of my head and into my heart and I was healed."

He looked at me and asked, "Young man, where do you live and what do you do for a living?" I replied that I was a chiropractor and lived in a small town in northern New Jersey. Few people have ever heard of our town, Waldwick, which is why upon further inquiry I told him that I lived close to Paramus, Ridgewood and the Saddle River area. Most people know Paramus because of all the shopping malls, Ridgewood because of the Valley Hospital and fine restaurants and Saddle River for the extreme wealth and fancy homes. So my jaw dropped when he got up from his chair and came closer to me and said, "I bet you live in Waldwick."

After I said a startled "Yes," he gave me a bear hug and exclaimed that he'd been the mayor of Waldwick and had lived there for many years before leaving to study the ministry! I never expected to hear that he was my town's former mayor. I had moved there and started my practice in 1974, and he'd left four years earlier, but this synchronicity we shared was an energetic sign to me that I was in the right place at that moment and had been meant to meet this man who healed himself and followed his bliss.

The way I found my way to Waldwick is another "chance encounter." During the summer before my graduation from college my mother had been camping at the family campgrounds in Harriman State Park called Lake Welch. Like me, my mom loved to talk to complete strangers, so as she was washing her dishes at the central water area she started up a conversation with a fellow camper who, they soon discovered, was a long lost cousin who shared the same Aunt Tilley. My mom mentioned that I was about to graduate from chiropractic college and was interested in settling somewhere in New Jersey. Her "cousin" told her to have me contact her husband, a local realtor, who would show me around. We did contact him, bought the second house he showed us and I have been practicing there for over forty-one years! The house, though not yet completely finished, was a perfect fit for us. Zoned for a home/office – provided the practitioner lived in the home – it had just the right amount of office space on the first floor and all the living space we could ever need on the second floor. I started my practice there on November 4th, 1974, three years to the day from when my son, Ryan, was born. Thank you, Mom, for your gift of gab!

Getting back to the story of meeting the former Waldwick mayor, Emmet Johnson, I met him on a Saturday, and the following Tuesday, while back home in Waldwick getting my hair cut at nearby Ho Ho Kus, I asked my barber, Dominic, if he'd ever heard of Emmet and did he know him. Dominic's barber shop was very well known and popular in the area, and as fate would have it, on deck to get his hair cut was the Waldwick Chief of Police, Danny Lupo. He'd overheard my question and replied that Emmet was, in fact, the former Waldwick mayor and he knew him very well. The Chief shared that when he was a rookie cop, on the first week of the job, there was a call for help to which he responded to the Johnson home. A tear flowed down his cheek as he relayed that Emmet's newborn son had died in Donny's arms on the way to the hospital! I was speechless, pondering the synchronicity of meeting both Emmet and the Chief. Through "coincidence" my Mom helped me find my home, and by chance, over a cup of tea, I met the former mayor of my town and had his identification confirmed soon afterward at the local barber shop! One just never knows when and where these "chance" meetings will play out in their future. Like my mother, I carry an open heart and intention to fulfill a higher destiny, and the universe always supports it!

Fast-forward some three decades later, and I had another encounter with Emmet, whom I call EJ. I would have to describe this unplanned encounter as a *super-synchronicity* event. It was on November 5th, 2019, the day we voted at our local town administration building. While waiting in line to cast my vote I noticed that the walls of the voting administration room were entirely covered with pictures of all the previous mayors from the past sixty years.

I had been voting in that room for the past forty-five years, but for some "unknown" reason had never noticed them. This election day I was compelled to check them out to see if EJ's picture might be among them. I walked around the entire room, only to discover his photo near the entryway. I took a photo of it with my iPhone and told the staff at the registration desk about my original synchronicity story – when and how I had met EJ at Lake Mohonk some three decades before. The story was fresh in my memory; I had just rewritten it for this book because for some "unknown" reason it had been missing from the original manuscript.

Several days prior to voting, while getting my hair cut at Dominic's barber shop where the original synchronicity occurred, Dominic had asked me, "Ken, how is the book coming along?" I told him it was going well. However, when I returned home to see if I could copy the story from the manuscript and give it to him for his personal use, I discovered it was missing! I was very upset and sat down to rewrite it on the spot and resubmit it to my publisher for inclusion in the book.

Right after I took the photo and told the story to the staff, none other than EJ, and his wife, walked into the room. I didn't recognize him as he had aged thirty years and was now ninety-five, but one of the older staff members identified him and said, "Dr. Harris, you're not going to believe me when I tell you to turn around and that man walking towards you is none other than EJ himself with his wife alongside him."

I was completely shocked but very excited to see him still alive and living in my town. I approached him and reintroduced myself as the person who had met him some decades before at Lake Mohonk, and much to my delight and surprise he said, "Yes, you are the chiropractor I met at Mohonk and who has an office down on East Prospect Street!"

The women at the registration desk witnessing this event unfolding were speechless and as surprised as I. One woman, being skeptical, asked how I had arranged for EJ to come in just as I finished telling them the story. Had I paid him to spook them as an April-Fool-like prank? I replied, "I did not arrange this meeting." She asked, "Then who did?" I answered that it must have been God!

I would never have recognized him by his appearance for he had lost about five inches in height, was walking with the aid of a cane and was somewhat stooped over. He did not resemble the man I had met some three decades earlier who had picked me up in a bear-like hug when he discovered I lived in Waldwick. But his cognition was intact and he remembered our original meeting. He told me he was now retired from the ministry but still owned homes in upstate New York and locally in Waldwick. When he retired from the ministry he decided to move back to Waldwick where he had family, friends and roots.

Life sought fit to reconnect us after so many years in a most exciting and totally unexpected way. I had decided to vote at the last minute on my way home from the dentist's office for some emergency dental repair. I had deviated from my normal practice of voting early in the day to avoid the nighttime rush; the dental visit required me to change my schedule and routine. Why I noticed the pictures on the wall and decided to take a photo of his picture minutes before he entered the room is part of the mystery. Why I decided to tell the staff the story of how I met him, and finished telling it at precisely the exact moment he was walking into the room, is beyond coincidence. Life is intelligent and can be trusted, and it has a way of connecting us – or in this case reconnecting us – at just the right time and place, much to our mutual surprise and delight. I promised him a signed copy of the book once published, and he said he looked forward to reading it. In real estate it's location, location, location; but in life it's timing, timing, timing!

GUIDANCE FROM BEYOND –
MY FATHER'S STORY

Sometimes I just look up, smile and say,
"I know that was you, God! Thanks!"
—unknown

My dad suffered from both clinical depression and heart disease, and was hospitalized several times during his life. The last time he succumbed to congestive heart failure, it was required that he be transferred to a long-term nursing facility. There was nothing more the staff at the local hospital could do for him and they said we would need to either take him home to die or get him placed in hospice at a long-term care facility. The problem was that at the time there were no available beds in the nursing homes in the area.

My aging mom was not in great physical or emotional shape and could not care for my dad at home. Because our financial resources were limited, we had to find a facility that accepted Medicare and Medicaid as payment in full for his residency. This was no easy task, and we were getting ongoing pressure from the hospital to take him out, since they were losing money on his care every day.

I researched local facilities and spent day and night visiting them and trying to get him placed, all to no avail! They all had very long waiting lists and a limited number of beds for charity cases, AKA Medicaid cases.

After a week of relentless inquiries and visits, I went to bed exhausted and quite despondent. That night I had a dream in which I was told to ask "John" for help with this dilemma. When I woke up, I mentioned to Judy that someone named John was going to help us, but *John who?* I wondered.

It was mid-December of 1996, and despite our personal family challenges we needed to make at least some preparations for the upcoming holiday season. We usually purchased our Christmas tree from one nursery and our annual poinsettia plants from another, but because of the ongoing stress and my lack of sleep, I decided to buy everything at the one nursey to save some time and energy.

While Judy picked out her plants I went outside to buy our tree. As I was looking over the trees I noticed someone I knew next to me doing the same. His name was John, and his son had had a teenaged romance with my daughter in high school. Because he was a man of community influence as president of the Bergen County Republican Party, I thought maybe he knew someone who could help us. He asked me how the family was doing, since it had been several years since we had spoken or seen one another. I told him my tale of woe regarding my father's health and the need for a nursing home placement. He finished listening to my story, smiled and said, "Well, Ken, perhaps I can be of help. I own two nursing homes. Here is the name of my administrator – give her call."

The next day I called, and two days later my dad was placed in one of his facilities! My dad lived in the nursing home for another eighteen months before he passed on, despite having received from the doctors at the hospital the prognosis of having three months or less to live.

At his memorial service at his church I had the privilege of saying some words to the congregation along with the local pastor. In preparation for this, I had asked my mom where I could find our needlepoint Star of David with the word *Shalom* printed on it. I wanted to place it on the altar for the service as a reminder of my father's life. *Shalom* is a Hebrew word that means hello, goodbye and peace. My mom could not remember where she put it, and in her emotional state I did not want to pressure her to look for it. But as I became still, a voice spoke to me saying that the needlepoint was upstairs in a box behind some packages, and indeed it was.

Guidance from beyond proved once again very helpful. Spirit can speak to us in a variety of ways. Sometimes it speaks to us in feelings and other times in dreams. We just have to stay alert and listen.

RECONNECTING WITH DR. WAYNE DYER

This is called synchronicity – a state in which you almost feel as if you are in a collaborative arrangement with fate.
—Wayne Dyer

When we were on another vacation in beautiful Maui, I had a series of experiences that defy logic or reason. Every morning Judy and I would take our usual walk before breakfast to start our day. As we were walking on the path outside our hotel, which parallels the beach, I looked ahead and saw, much to my surprise, a lifetime mentor of mine coming towards us from the opposite direction.

Dr. Wayne Dyer was on his cell phone as he approached, and I could not contain myself. I shouted out a loud good morning greeting. He mysteriously dropped his phone and lost the cell connection, and suddenly we had time to engage one another in a brief conversation.

I reminded him that we had met some fifteen years prior at a seminar in northern California and that we had taken a photo together, which was still in my possession. I said he had looked at me after the photo was taken and said, "Ken, it feels like you and I share one heart." I had never forgotten the feeling and what he said to me. He has always been an inspiration in my journey in consciousness and I have read all his books and listened to all his CDs over many years. Meeting him this way was, to say the least, a dream come true. I asked Judy to take another photo of us and we once again embraced each other, side by side, the way we had in our first photo.

After a short conversation, we continued our respective walks in opposite directions. About half an hour later our paths crossed again. He was looking for me, and this time he said he had been told by God that I could help him. He said he needed help with some physical health challenges he had been experiencing over the past year. He knew from our first encounter that I was a chiropractor and he asked if I would be open and available to check him out chiropractically. I agreed, and we arranged for me to go to his home the following day. What occurred after I adjusted him was quite remarkable. We shared an energetic session known as an *Attunement*. He fell asleep during that session, and upon awakening he said he felt like he had been taken into a heavenly state of consciousness.

When I got back to the hotel, I went to the breakfast buffet. I served myself, sat down with my food and took out a book by Dr. Caroline Myss entitled *Why People Don't Heal and How They Can*. A woman sitting next to me noticed the book and engaged me in conversation. She asked if I was familiar with other works by Caroline Myss. I responded yes and that I had spent four days with her and Dr. Norm Shealy in Chicago a few weeks prior.

She said that she had noticed me reading the book on the airplane to Maui and had intended to speak with me but lost track of me after we landed. Here we now found ourselves staying at the same hotel and eating breakfast together.

After a brief conversation, she told me that she was a nurse and a massage therapist and owned a wellness center in upstate New York. She mentioned that she had come to Maui for two reasons. First, she planned to attend a five-day workshop at another hotel with Ram Dass, Krishna Das, and Sharon Salzburg. I was familiar with all three presenters and told her about our intention of attending a public concert with Krishna Das that very same evening.

Her second reason for visiting Maui was because her mother had recently passed on and had given her many books and tapes of someone named Wayne Dyer! She asked me if I was familiar with his work and I said yes, very familiar, and in fact had just some fifteen minutes earlier met him on the path outside our hotel. Her eyes filled up with tears and she told me she had had a premonition that she, too, would "run into him on the path somewhere in Maui" but didn't know exactly where, when or how it might work out for her to meet him.

I said I was to meet with him at his condo the very next day and would relay the story to him and see if he was open to meeting with her. The next day I told Wayne about the encounter, and as I was leaving after our healing session he said he was going to call her later in the day and meet her. Later that morning I saw the two of them walking on the path speaking to each other on cell phones about twenty feet apart. They did in fact meet, and her premonition came true and materialized just the way she had seen it in her mind.

A week later Judy and I planned to visit the island of Kauai. While at the airport lounge waiting for our flight, we planned our next summer vacation to Canada. We had always wanted to hike the Canadian Rockies; we had already hiked in most of the US national parks. Judy said we should fly into Calgary and drive up to the Rockies from there.

Just then a nice-looking couple sat down next to us in the lounge. I heard the woman say something to her husband using the expression "Eh" and a certain way of saying "about." I smiled and said, "Hey, you guys talk funny! You must be from Canada!" They said yes, from Calgary! We engaged in some friendly conversation and after about twenty minutes the woman asked me out of the blue if I had ever heard of a man named Wayne Dyer. Well, for a second I almost thought that Wayne had put her up to it and sent her to the airport as a lark. No, it was not a setup. Claudette and her husband, Larry, had gone up to Haleakala that very morning to see the sun rise above the clouds, and her prayer was to meet Dr. Dyer. It manifested later that day upon returning from the volcano and she had a photo to prove it!

When Judy and I returned home from Maui, I went to pick up the box of accumulated mail and was so tired from all the hours of travel, I dropped it on the floor. The first thing that stood out in the pile was a magazine with Wayne's photo on the front cover and the caption "Dr. Wayne Dyer – Spiritual Hero for 2012"! It seemed as if he had followed me home, for wherever I went or whomever I spoke to would ask me if I knew him!

Wait; it gets better. My first week back, one of my patients came to my office for an adjustment wearing a headset. I informed her that she would have to shut off the set while being adjusted and she looked at me and asked had I heard Wayne Dyer's new book on tape,

Wishes Fulfilled? This was a book Wayne had signed and given me just before Judy and I left Maui.

More recently, one day I woke up extra early feeling compelled to revise and enhance the preface to this book. I checked my email and had received one from Hay House addressed to me and signed posthumously by Wayne. I immediately opened it and read it, and felt I was being guided. Hay House was offering an online training program and I decided to sign up on the spot. I had been struggling with how to go about finding a literary agent to represent me to publishers. A new friend of mine, musician and poet Bob Sima, had just produced and released his latest CD entitled *It's Time*, which I often listen to in the morning in preparation for my morning meditation. I love the entire album because each and every song carries an uplifting spiritual message, especially the track called "Meditation Is the Medication Which Breaks the Illusion of Separation." So when I saw the email message "It's time!" I knew I was being guided. Because I signed that day, I saved $300 off the seminar price and received many added benefits, not the least of which were some online videos of Wayne himself!

They say everything is connected, and this string of events proves the point. We are all part of the web of life and these coincidences are happening all the time and we must be open and alert to realize this spiritual truth: All is One!

Experiencing Oneness

At the eighteenth annual International Society for the Study of Subtle Energy and Energy Medicine (ISSSEEM) conference held in Boulder, Colorado, I was privileged, along with some 450 other participants, to receive the Deeksha Blessing by one of our keynote presenters, the former TV and movie actress Lindsay Wagoner, who was best known for her role as the Bionic Woman.

I had met Lindsay that Thursday afternoon at lunch on the patio of the hotel restaurant. One of my best friends, Dr. Ken Lim, and I were exchanging sacred objects when out of the corner of my eye I saw Lindsay observing us as we performed a ritual blessing on one another. My eyes met hers momentarily and she was looking at us with smiling, wide-open eyes as we exchanged our gifts to one another.

Ken had brought back for me from New Zealand, his home country, a jade pendant depicting the Maori mythological creature Manaia. I had traveled one year prior with Ken to Peru along with sixteen others on a spiritual pilgrimage to the sacred mountain of Machu Picchu and brought back with me a Peruvian cross which I gave him. After our lunch and brief ceremony we went over to Lindsay's table, and when I saw her name tag I remembered that she was a keynote speaker scheduled to speak the following Monday on the subject of "Calm Mind – Open Heart." She asked us if we had heard of the Oneness Blessing and the Deeksha process, and I had to admit that I had not. She told us a little about her work with battered women in the Los Angeles County jail system and her attempts to offer service and blessing as part of the rehabilitation program there.

On Monday morning Lindsay took the stage and spoke of her work and connection to the Oneness University and the Oneness Blessing process. Then she offered this blessing to all 450 of us, en masse. Along with others I went forward and lay down for the process in the posture known as the Dead Man's Pose. I had made a conscious choice to be open to receiving despite my skepticism and aversion to anything associated with guruism. During the process, although my eyes were closed, my heart remained wide open and the music provided a beautiful atmosphere in which this process was received.

At the conclusion of the blessing we returned to our seats and Lindsay explained that this transmission of energy was given to her by the founders of the Oneness University, Sri Amma and Bhagavan. She invited anyone who wished to line up outside the conference room and meet her personally if so moved.

She was not signing her book since it hadn't yet been published, but was open to meeting anyone.

Many of us lined up and waited our turn, and when I approached her I felt compelled to bow to her and saluted her with the Sanskrit salutation *Namaste*, which means "I see and acknowledge the Divine in you that is in me and we are one." I then asked permission to hug her in appreciation of the blessing, and we embraced.

What happened next caught me by complete surprise. As we pressed our heart spaces to one another, my heart literally stopped for a nanosecond and then matched the beat, cadence and rhythm of hers! For what seemed like a long time we were beating as *one heart*!

I had never had quite this experience of visceral Oneness with anyone else in my sixty-one years on this earth journey. I practice a spiritual form of energy work called Attunement, and have experienced vibrational connections with clients in which our energy fields merged, but never in quite the same way as in this experience with Lindsay. Her heart and mine were actually beating as one heart! Needless to say I was quite taken aback and surprised by this encounter. The Deeksha transmission was for me very real and tangible.

The feeling of calmness and peace stayed with me for several days. I haven't personalized this energy with Lindsay and I'm not romantically in love with her, but I'm most thankful to her for the experience of Deeksha she provided for the attendees of the conference. Blessings right back to you, Lindsay, and may you continue to bless all who come to know and connect with you and the divine energy of Oneness we all share!

Timing and Synchronicity

I once treated a psychotherapist who was undergoing psychoanalysis with a new psychiatrist. She wanted me to meet her doctor, thinking we might develop a referral relationship with one another since we both embraced a holistic approach to treatment and could benefit from getting to know one another. I was busy with my chiropractic practice as well as developing my mind-body wellness center, and didn't have much free time to meet her doctor, so I politely said, "If I'm supposed to meet this doctor, the universe will arrange it down the road." This was on a Friday, and unbeknownst to me, while dining at The Freelance Cafe in Piedmont, New York, the following weekend, I did meet this person.

Judy and I always enjoyed walking by the Hudson River before eating at the Freelance. On that Friday it was completely full so we decided to try a new restaurant down the block called The Turning Point. The host led us to the last remaining seats. We would have preferred to sit downstairs where live music was being played, but we were so hungry we decided to stay.

I'm a sociable person so it was not long before the man at the next table and I hit it off and discovered we shared much in common, especially things metaphysical. Judy and the woman with him didn't say much during this conversation. They told us they lived near the restaurant and dined there often to enjoy the music but also liked to sit upstairs where it was more intimate.

When we left, the man and I exchanged business cards and I politely asked the woman what she did. She said she enjoyed art and poetry but didn't mention what type of work she did. I handed her my card and asked her to please send me her business card for my files.

The following Monday, as I was waiting for my last morning patient – the same psychotherapist I mentioned earlier – I got my mail from the mailbox. I was opening an envelope when she arrived, and a business card fell to the floor, and when I picked it up I told her that I'd met this nice couple over the weekend and here was this woman's business card stating that she was a psychiatrist. I had assumed she was an artist! When I showed my patient the card, she exclaimed, "That's my new doctor whom I wanted you to meet!"

The couple became our friends and attended our twenty-fifth anniversary celebration soon afterward.

The doctor became a patient of mine and we developed a professional, collaborative relationship. Apparently the universe was working out all the details for us to meet, and in this case sooner than later!

MY COUSIN "JACK"

> *Your vibe will attract your tribe.*
> *—unknown*

L ast year I reconnected with my uncle, Nat Rand, to whom I am related through the marriage of my mother's sister, Margaret Rand. Uncle Nat is in his nineties and had been asked by his grandchildren to answer questions about their family history. He decided to do some research, and over a ten-year period compiled a family tree. Since he was married to my mother's sister, his children and I shared some common family history.

Upon reading the memoirs I discovered much to my dismay that the history of the Tietgen side of my family reveals some unsavory alleged facts based on stories told to my uncle by my grandmother, Catherine Carr. According to his research on the Mormon LDS Church's database, my maternal grandfather, Frank Tietgen, was somehow related to the Pierre Laval family from France. My uncle incorrectly concluded that Frank Tietgen's mother was Marie Laval from France, who was the sister of Pierre Laval, the Prime Minister of France during the Vichy government under Nazi Germany's rule during World War II. This alleged connection to the despot was somewhat unsettling to me. Laval was tried, convicted and shot by a firing squad for collaborating with the Germans and was responsible for sending many Jews to the death camps. Boy, was I upset to read that!

Shortly after I read those memoirs, a new patient came to my office who was an expert in genealogy. I asked her to research this alleged fact as I could not believe that my mother's family came from such a history of disgrace. The genealogist told me not to despair; that in her experience verbal accounts get mixed up from generation to generation and she would get to the truth by obtaining a marriage certificate from the state of New Jersey that would show who my grandmother's and grandfather's parents were. Once obtained, she assured me, she could trace back through census records to when they emigrated to America.

After a six-week delay the documents finally arrived. The marriage certificate showed that Frank Tietgen's parents were Henry Tietgen and Margaret

Cosgrove, who emigrated from Germany and Ireland respectively. So Marie Laval from France was *not* related to us! I was so relieved to find out the truth of my ancestry.

In the course of researching the family tree, the genealogist made a notation online regarding her inquiry into the Tietgen family history. Several weeks later I got a phone call from someone in Utah who claimed he saw the notation and that he was in fact a second cousin of mine since he and I both had the same great-grandparents. He told me that according to his research there were additional family members in Bayonne, New Jersey, where my mother was born, and that they shared the same great-grandparents. And he said there was another chiropractor in the family named John Smith, who practices in Bayonne to this very day.

I immediately got John Smith's information and called his office. I asked him if he had the same great-grandparents and he said yes. I asked him where he attended chiropractic college and he informed me that he went to Life University in Atlanta, Georgia, a school I helped promote support for back in the 1970s.

I asked him if he knew my very best friend, Dr. Bob Rabin, whom I had inspired and sent to Life University. He said that he knew him well and was in fact a fellow classmate and in his graduating class in 1980. John then told me that after five years of practicing chiropractic he decided to go back to medical school and had had a family medicine practice in Bayonne, where he was born, for over twenty years.

I called my friend Bob and he did in fact know John Smith, but not as John but rather as Jack. He knew him as a former policeman from New Jersey and described him as a big fellow of 6'4", built like a New Jersey Giants football player. This description fit John, AKA Jack, to a T!

Jack and I arranged to meet the following week at his office. We both pulled up to his office at exactly the same time to discover that we both drove the same car – color, make and model! When I got out of my vehicle to greet him, I was awestruck by his physical appearance. He looked more like my mother than I did! His hair color, blue eyes and the shape of his face were just like my mom's. He said he was surprised to see that I looked like his first cousins the Forests, and that if he had seen me in a crowd somewhere he would have come over to ask if I was related to them. I was a dead ringer for their family!

Jack and I spent the next five hours driving around Bayonne. He showed me where my grandfather had lived and worked as well as the church where my mom was baptized and went to school. It was somewhat surreal for me to visit the places of my ancestors' births. I discovered that the oil refinery where my grandfather worked was no longer there and the home in which he was born was now occupied by a new wave of immigrants.

Jack said that one of our aunts was still alive and well at age ninety-two, living in Bayonne, and that she would know a lot about the family history. Her name is Leona Forest, the mother of the cousins I resembled according to Jack. I called her on the phone and set up a time to meet to go over the family tree together, sharing whatever information and pictures I had with her.

Funny how life works. I had had no interest in my genealogy prior to reading the memories about my maternal family tree, although my mother did tell me when she was alive that she grew up in Bayonne and that some of her relatives were in the policeman department. Jack told me that his brother, Mark Smith, is the director of the Bayonne police department. I spoke to Mark briefly that day and he sounded excited to discover our connection and looked forward to meeting me soon to compare notes with me as well.

I told Jack that our great-grandparents, Henry Tietgen and Margaret Cosgrove, were surely smiling in heaven over our "chance" reconnection, and we both agreed that we felt like we were old friends meeting again after a long time of separation.

So much might be said for the energy of DNA regarding physical similarities and shared memories. Native Americans, indigenous Africans and Aboriginal peoples believe that everyone in your bloodline lives in your DNA memory field, and after having met Jack I believe that to be true. To be continued…

THE RETURNING HEART

Between thinking and seeing,
there is a place called knowing.
—*Caroline Myss*

In June of 2007 I traveled to one of the world's seven wonders, known as Machu Picchu, along with sixteen other adventurous souls from all around the US. We were all called to visit this magical place for different reasons, and under the leadership of Dr. Deb Sandella of Colorado, spent seventeen days visiting in Peru's Sacred Valley. This was a most magical and spiritual time for me. I earlier described how it came about in the story "A Call to the Mountain."

Prior to meeting in Lima, we were asked by Deb to bring something of spiritual meaning with us that we were to offer to someone on our trip as a "giveaway" exchange after our sunrise winter solstice experience on Machu Picchu.

I chose to take a pink heart-shaped quartz stone that called to me while browsing at a shop in Rhinebeck, New York. I knew this was what I was supposed to take with me to the magic mountain. Its feminine color and the energy attached to it were perfect for Machu Picchu, which, according to folklore, is a place of heart and feminine spirit. Legend also has it that a woman is supposed to lead you to the top of the mountain, so my choice was just perfect, and I took this stone with me to Peru.

I did not know who I was going to give it to, but since Deb was to lead the way I felt compelled to give it to her as a sign of love and appreciation for her efforts in organizing the trip and leading us to this sacred site. I never discussed this part of my journey with Judy, since it was a personal choice for each one to make and did not feel relevant to the overall purpose and experience of the journey. The reason I mention this is that one year later Judy attended a one-week Emotional Freedom Seminar with Deepak Chopra at the La Costa Spa in Carlsbad, California. At the conclusion of the week each participant was given a pink heart-shaped stone identical to the one I had given away in Machu Picchu one year earlier.

When I reconnected with Judy after her time in Carlsbad, I was also in California attending the Annual

Attunement Guild session in Corona. The first thing she gave me after our week apart was this stone, *identical* to the one I had given away! And she prefaced giving me the gift by saying that for some unknown reason everyone in attendance received one, but she found *two* in her bag and wanted to give me the extra one in love and appreciation.

I was almost speechless, and then told her that I had given the same stone to our group leader the year prior as part of my Machu Picchu experience, for the same reason. My heart was returning to me, completing the circle in a most unexpected and beautiful way!

Upon returning home I called Deb and she assured me that the one I had given to her was still on her altar in Colorado and had not traveled back to New Jersey!

They say nothing has any meaning except the meaning you give it. What might be the significance of this moving forward is speculative and can take on many interpretations from merely statistical coincidence to angelic manipulation. Who knows? I leave it to you to fill in the possible explanations, but I choose to see this event and the symbolic heart-shaped stone as my love returning to me along with the feminine energy it carried in its molecular vibration.

A MEANINGFUL ENCOUNTER

> *No one is sent by accident to anyone.*
> *—A Course in Miracles*

Judy and I enjoy walking in one of several parks close to our home to avoid the traffic and exhaust fumes in our local neighborhood. Upon recently returning from a month-long vacation in Florida, we decided to take a walk in a nearby Glen Rock, New Jersey, park. We have been walking there for many years, and took our now-grown children there with their bikes, as there is a dedicated bike path.

On this day we decided, due to the cold and wind, to take the park's shorter walking path around a small pond. There are many memorial benches on this path where you can stop and rest.

About two blocks from the park entrance is a very large and beautiful Sikh temple attended by large crowds on the weekends. I secretly always wanted to visit but had reservations and concerns about doing so. In 2012 there was a tragic shooting event at a Wisconsin Sikh temple; a deranged white supremacist, thinking the Sikhs were of Arabic descent, shot and killed six people and injured many others. Because of that event I was reluctant to just show up for fear that my appearance as a white Caucasian male might evoke fear in the congregation, so I never attempted to make a visit.

While we were walking around the park that day, two young males dressed in traditional Sikh attire came alongside Judy and me. I'm not sure what prompted me to start a conversation with them, but I did. I asked, "Are you members of the temple a couple of blocks away?" to which they replied, "Yes, we are." I then proceeded to tell them that I was somewhat familiar with their religion because I had had the privilege and honor to host a Sikh couple from the Punjab region at my home many years ago. They had come to America to study in the spiritual community I was affiliated with. This was unusual in that it was more common for Americans to go to India in search of enlightenment and healing.

This couple found their way here because my mentor and teacher at the time, Dr. Bill Bahan, had performed what appeared to them as miraculous healing. He, like me, was trained as a traditional chiropractor but had gone on to study an energy healing technique called Attunement, which is a nonphysical method of touch that balances the endocrine glands by working in the *light body* (what some people call the *aura*, or energy field surrounding the body) of the individual. A famous and revered guru had lapsed into a coma and there was no likelihood that he would wake up, medically speaking; but he came out of the coma after receiving the Attunement from Dr. Bahan. This, of course, impressed many who witnessed the "miracle," and as a result word spread quickly and many came to the US to study this approach to healing.

The couple had just finished their training in America and I was asked to host them until their return to India. This was no ordinary couple. The man was a direct descendant of the founder of the Sikh religion, had been educated at Oxford and held the prestigious position as a general in the Gurkha army. They owned and operated a 200,000-acre tree farm and had great wealth and fame in the Punjab region.

After sharing this story with my newfound Sikh friends, one of them told me he had been there when the Wisconsin shootings occurred. His father was the head priest of the temple and on that day he was unfortunately shot in the face, became paralyzed and had been in a coma-like state ever since. I got goosebumps and asked him if I could hug him and we embraced each other! He then went on to tell me he was now the main priest at the gurudwara, or Sikh temple, in Glen Rock and that

I would be most welcome anytime to attend a service as his guest.

Funny how the universe brought us together at that point in time and space on a simple walk around the park! I don't know why I chose to speak to those men that day and share that particular story. I do plan to attend the temple service in the very near future, and perhaps I might be of some help to him and his father in offering to share an Attunement. I feel that our "chance" meeting was purposeful and could have been arranged by invisible forces as a blessing for all concerned.

SYNCHRODESTINY IN ACTION – WAYNE, DEEPAK AND OPRAH

An invisible thread connects those who are destined to meet, regardless of time, place and circumstance.
—Chinese proverb

Several years ago I had a vivid dream in which I saw myself being interviewed by Oprah Winfrey on her television station about a book I had written in which I told about meeting Deepak Chopra and Wayne Dyer while walking along a path near the ocean. Both events have happened as I saw them in my vivid dream state.

You've already read the story about how I met Wayne Dyer in Hawaii. My next synchronistic encounter, which Deepak Chopra termed *synchrodestiny*, happened not long after the first time I met Wayne in 1996 at a conference in Yosemite National Park. Immediately after meeting him, I left the conference in order to catch a flight from San Francisco to San Diego, intending to go to La Jolla and visit the famous Chopra Center, called the Chopra Center for Well Being at the time. I innately just knew that I would meet Dr. Chopra because in my dream, this, too, happened. The sponsor of the conference thought I was crazy and said I had little to no chance of meeting Deepak Chopra without a prearranged appointment.

Even though I had no appointment to meet him, I knew it was going to take place and was part of my destiny. I arrived in La Jolla, checked into the hotel, which was around the corner from the center, went up to my room, unpacked my belongings, went back down to the front desk and asked the clerk where the center was in relationship to the hotel. She replied, "Oh, it's just two blocks away," and all I had to do was go out the front door, make a right turn, go to the corner of the building, make another right turn and walk two blocks to the center.

You can imagine my excitement, surprise and delight when, as I made the right turn around the corner of the building, I almost knocked Deepak Chopra over! We literally collided into each other! I said how happy

I was to finally meet him in person and told him I had just left his friend Wayne up in northern California at a seminar. I added that the reason I had travelled to his center was to invite him to be our keynote presenter sometime in the future and to address a healthcare gathering at one of my favorite vacations spots in upstate New York, the Mohonk Mountain House. I showed him the brochure I had with me and he immediately got on his cell phone to check his schedule with his secretary and make room for me to visit with him the next day at his private office! He asked me if he could keep the brochure for his files as he was very interested in visiting this spectacular-looking place.

The next day I had the wonderful opportunity of spending a couple of hours alone with another one of my mentors in life. I had read all his books and found great resonance with his messages of healing, consciousness and spirituality. It was a dream come true.

As I was leaving I told him how honored I was to have met him and thanked him for reserving some private time in his already full schedule without any advance notice. I also expressed my admiration and respect for what he was doing to promote holistic healthcare in the US as well as around the world. I will never forget how he looked at me with love in his eyes and said, "May God bless you too, Ken, as you travel ahead with your vision and mission as well." I left feeling an overwhelming sense of gratitude and appreciation for what had just transpired between Deepak and me!

Okay, so two down – "chance" meetings with both Wayne and Deepak completed – and now one more to go and the precognitive dream will be complete. As of this writing, my meeting with Oprah has not yet occurred but I know I'm getting closer because I have now met two of her closest friends quite unexpectedly over the last two years.

At my favorite vacation spot over a July 4th holiday, I met Gayle King while on a short hike around a lake and told her of my dream about meeting Oprah and being interviewed on her Super Soul Sunday TV series. I also told her that I was two-thirds complete with my dream, having already met Wayne and Deepak. She smiled and replied, "Give me your business card and I'll personally give it to her and relay your dream to her. Oprah loves stories like this and perhaps may contact you at some future time for that interview." I thanked her and off we went in opposite directions on the walking path.

In March of the following year, while vacationing in La Jolla, I met Stedman Graham while eating breakfast at the La Jolla Hyatt. He literally sat right next to me without any prompting. I introduced myself and asked if Oprah was traveling with him at that time. He replied no, that he was on a business trip. He's a motivational speaker and travels to schools all over the world giving uplifting speeches hoping to elevate the self-esteem of young people everywhere. Stedman and Oprah have been a couple for years and often travel together to public events. When I told him my story about my dream, he, too, asked for my business card and said he would pass it along next time he saw Oprah.

I know it is only a question of when, not if, I will meet Oprah down the road. I just might send her a copy of this book, and who knows – I might be invited for that long overdue interview just as in my dream!

MIRACLE ON EAST
PROSPECT STREET

*Miracles happen every day. Not just in remote
country villages or at holy sites halfway across the
globe, but here, in our own lives.*
—Deepak Chopra

We have all heard of the movie *Miracle on 34th Street*, but my personal miracle took place in 2008 right on East Prospect Street in Waldwick, New Jersey, where I maintained a home/office setup for over forty-five years.

Judy wanted to clean our house for the upcoming holiday celebrations and decided to additionally clean the ashes from the second story fireplace in our family room. The night before we had enjoyed a fire that burned for several hours producing copious amounts of ash. The fire had been extinguished for about twelve hours, but Judy remarked to me that the ashes still felt somewhat warm. She nevertheless proceeded to diligently clean them out with a metal shovel and place them in a plastic garbage bag, then asked me to take them downstairs and put them in our twenty-five-gallon plastic garbage can.

Without thinking I placed the bag of what I thought were cold ashes into the garbage can, which we kept alongside our house next to a wooden fence and against the outside of our attached garage. This area was right under our wooden deck, which was a second-story structure wrapping around our entire house. Behind the fence we stored our seasoned firewood, which at that time amounted to about a half cord of wood. Right alongside this attached garage with cedar siding, we parked our second car outside in an alcove.

You get the picture by now. Lots of wood, all in a strategic area, setting the stage for a potential disaster should something ignite in this area by mistake.

It took about four hours before the unthinkable transpired. The smoldering ashes burst into flames. We could not see flames, but we certainly smelled something burning somewhere nearby, never thinking it originated from our home. Our front entrance did not face the side of our home, so our view was obscured.

Judy was leaving our house and told me something smelled like it was burning, and we both stepped outside and agreed that there must be a fire somewhere in the neighborhood, never thinking it was at our home!

She drove up the street to our local library and I went back to my office. Within minutes my neighbor came screaming across the street thinking that our car was on fire because that's where the flames appeared to be coming from. I looked around the corner of my home, and much to my disbelief saw the flames shooting out from the garbage can up alongside our house. The wooden fence in front of the garage was rapidly burning. I immediately realized that I must get my keys and move the parked car before it, too, ignited or exploded. It was parked right under the second story overhang and once on fire would surely have ignited the second story of our home.

I successfully moved the car and went back to see what, if anything, I could do about subduing the remaining fire, which was rapidly escalating and engulfing the back side of my home by now. Just then a passerby pulled into my driveway and asked if I had a fire extinguisher and what my address was. I told him yes, I did have an extinguisher, and gave him my address. He got on his cell and called 911.

I returned from upstairs with the extinguisher and he took it from me and proceeded to douse the flames and asked me if I had a water hose anywhere nearby. While he was using the fire extinguisher, I quickly reconnected a garden hose which had been turned off for the winter. Once I got the hose reconnected I realized the firewood pile, which was stacked immediately behind the fence, was in jeopardy of catching fire, and pushed the entire half cord of wood away from the shooting flames. I then joined the good Samaritan and pumped copious amounts of water on the fire and house shingles.

I will never forget the feeling of heat and the sound of the fire. The smell and smoke generated from the burning garbage and plastic bottles was overpowering at one point, causing me to move back from the flames. We got it under control just as the fire trucks and police arrived and took over from us. I'm convinced that had we not fought this fire, my entire house would have been engulfed in flames by the time the fire department arrived, which took about fifteen minutes from the time the gentleman called. The firemen used their hoses on the house and went through my house to the garage to shut off the electrical supply and cut two holes in the ceiling of the garage. They then used a heat-sensitive video camera to make sure that no fire had penetrated the outside wall. They were checking to see if any smoldering embers were inside the walls that might later ignite the insulation. Luckily no hot spots were discovered.

These events took place in what felt like a surreal time warp for me. I remember saying to myself as I was hooking up the water hose, *If this doesn't work in the next thirty seconds, let it go and move away, as the whole house is about to catch fire and it would be beyond me and this good Samaritan to contain this raging firestorm.* And had Judy and I gone out for lunch, as we often do, we would have returned home to *no* home, for the fire would surely have consumed our house.

It was all divine intervention for sure, and no coincidence in my mind. We never found out who the unknown passerby was who helped put out the fire. No one in the fire department or the police department could identify him from the description I gave. The universe steps in at times when we most need it if we stay open to the possibility of "miracles."

NO "COINCIDENCE" HERE!

In the tapestry of life, we're all connected.
Each one of us is a gift to those around us,
helping each other to be who we are.
—*Anita Moorjani*

After a recent teleconference with Dr. Lissa Rankin, I decided to reach out to her and offer my help in getting more men involved in her Whole Health Medicine Institute. I had attended a conference she had organized a few years prior at which I was the *only* male participant in a prestigious group of fifty-five women practitioners, many of whom were traditionally trained and educated medical doctors; the rest were alternative healthcare providers.

Dr. Rankin had left a traditional medical practice some years before and was now concentrating her energy and efforts on helping to reform the current dehumanizing and broken healthcare system by training practitioners to consider perspectives that include body, mind and spirit. She has written several best-sellers and did some extremely popular TED Talks discussing a new paradigm for modern healthcare to make it more humane for doctor and patient alike.

In my email I told her that I was a graduate of the Mankind Project, an all-male organization that runs weekend training programs for the purpose of restoring sacred masculinity in the hearts and minds of men who are looking for more meaning and purpose in their lives. Many of the men in this nationwide organization have degrees, licenses, and training in the healing arts. I felt it would be a perfect place to introduce Dr. Rankin's work and perhaps motivate more men to join her organization to help balance out the male/female ratio. I asked her if she had ever heard of the Mankind Project.

Dr. Rankin responded and, noting my connection to the Mankind Project, said that to her delight and surprise, her new husband of just seven weeks was a graduate of the program and felt it had had a profound life-changing effect and influence on him!

We have now begun the process of masterminding and networking to see just how we may join forces and have the Mankind Project and the Whole Health Medicine Institute collaborate on some programs down the road. Again, no "coincidence" here, and I interpret it as the universe wanting this collaboration to happen.

BEYOND COINCIDENCE

> *I believe there are no random meetings in our lives —*
> *that everyone we touch, who touches us, has been put*
> *in our path for a reason.*
> —*Susanna Kearsley*

One Friday after I'd finished my morning hours at my office, I stayed late to copy some papers that my accountant had requested earlier in the day. Normally our morning hours would end around 12:30 or 12:45, so I turned off the lights and for all appearances the office looked closed.

At 1:10 I heard a car pull into the parking lot. I recognized the driver as a patient, and when he got out of the car I could see by the way he was standing that he needed my services. I hesitated for a moment and questioned whether to open the door or pretend I wasn't in. After all, it was my lunch hour, and time was getting short before I would need to return for afternoon hours.

I decided to open the door, and greeted the man warmly. When he realized that the office was closed, he apologized for the intrusion and offered to come back during regular office hours. I quickly assured him that it was no problem and took him into my office to see what I could do to help him.

The patient, a policeman, told me he'd had a difficult night on the job. He'd responded to an auto accident and had helped extricate two young men from a serious collision. He had been bent over for an hour and a half in one position, supporting one of the trapped victims. Soon after workers created enough space to move the man the officer was supporting, the man hemorrhaged and died in his arms. The officer, who was also a CPR instructor, tried desperately to save him, but to no avail. The young man died despite all energy and efforts.

The emotional trauma the officer had suffered was obvious. I asked him if he'd had an opportunity to grieve and release the tension through crying. He indicated that he had not. I quietly placed him face down on the adjusting table and prepared him for an adjustment. I placed one hand on the back of his head and the other on his lower back, closed my eyes, found a still point of focus and shared an Attunement with this patient. After several moments of stillness between us, his irregular breathing changed to sighs. Then, quickly, came deep crying. In stillness I allowed what needed to be released to be let go.

After several more minutes I helped him sit upright and spoke to him gently in words of consolation and understanding. A healing had occurred between us. We returned to the reception room, and while we were talking I opened the door to greet another of my patients and invited her in. As they passed each other, they exchanged greetings; one entered, the other left.

This second patient seemed pale and distraught. I took her into the adjusting room and asked her what was wrong. She began to tell me of a close friend with whom she used to work. Her friend's two sons had been involved in a serious car accident the night before. One son had died and the other was still in critical condition. She said that as she was passing my office she felt compelled to come in. The news of the accident had created such an emotional reaction that her neck and back felt strained and tense, and she knew immediately that we could help reduce her tension.

As life would have it, I soon discovered that these two patients were part of the same event. The police officer who had just left the office was the one who'd attended the two sons of the second patient's friend. Here we were, all involved in the outcome of this event. I adjusted her and advised her to bring comfort and healing to her longtime friend.

We shouldn't be surprised when these so-called coincidences occur, for one Spirit is in operation in everyone, everywhere. The conscious mind could not have arranged all the factors involved to result in such a synchronicity as this. Spirit, invisible yet tangible, was at work orchestrating all the various factors necessary for our paths to cross and to touch and bless one another. Both patients had felt compelled to come to the office within minutes of each other even though neither had appointments and the office was actually closed. Although I had been treating both for several years, they had never met in my office before.

I never met the woman whose sons had been in the accident but, having been privileged to touch these two patients, I felt connected to her through them. Life has a magic all its own. I'm glad that my accountant called that morning, and I'm thankful I stayed late and responded to the need at hand. Opportunities to serve do come continuously and unexpectedly.

NEVER SAY NEVER – A SYNCHRONISTIC JOURNEY THROUGH FEAR TO HEALING

Synchronicity holds the promise that if we want to change inside, the patterns of our external life will change as well.
—Jean Shinoda Bolen

They say to avoid using words like *never* and *always*. This is my personal story of healing in which the string of synchronicities revealed left me quite astounded.

It all started very innocently two years ago when I fell in my own backyard. I had walked down the stairs from my deck onto a slate walkway covered with some moss and wet from light rain. After a few steps I found myself airborne, landing with a traumatic impact on my left side, back and hip. Because I could not immediately move, I thought at first that I might have broken my hip. I felt stunned and not quite sure how I had gotten from walking to lying on the ground. But after several moments lying there I was able to roll over and get myself up! Little did I know at that time that this fall was to have some very dire consequences and lesson-learning for me down the road; it would take two more years for this fall to forever change my life.

Having been a chiropractor for forty-plus years, I knew how important it was that I get my spine checked and adjusted to restore my alignment soon after the fall. Off I went to my local DC to get adjusted the very same day.

Several weeks later I noticed that my gait felt off during my early morning walks in the park. Something was just not quite right.

After several more months of still feeling not quite right, I decided to get an MRI of my hips to rule out any possible hairline fracture or pathology. The MRI came back negative, showing only some inflammation in muscle tissue consistent with trauma from the fall as well as a small cyst.

What I did not find out at that time was that the fall ruptured the synovial membrane at my L4 joint, forcing it to tear and leak internally into my spinal canal. This would come back to haunt me, but it would take some time for the pain to show up, worsen and not respond to the treatments I was trying – everything from chiropractic to massage, acupuncture, reiki, faith healing and nutritionists – all to no avail.

I saw an orthopedist who said my problem was age-related and I was suffering from spinal stenosis. He said everything I was doing was okay, but if my pain continued he could give me epidural injections to help. I politely refused and resumed the treatment protocols I had been doing. This worked well for an additional six months, and then the condition worsened and the pain became intolerable.

I then consulted with a second orthopedist who asked for a second MRI to compare to the first one taken almost a year before. The results showed that the cyst had doubled in size and was now filling up the entire left side of my neural canal. He suggested I follow up with a neurosurgeon who had experience with this type of condition. I was about to do something I had vowed never to do because I had seen the sometimes devastating results of spinal surgery, like paralysis and death: consult with a neurosurgeon for possible spinal surgery.

Now the search began to find someone I trusted and who could perform this type of surgery safely – as if any spinal surgery is considered safe! After putting out feelers to friends and associates, I remembered I had a friend who was a general surgeon at St. Luke's Roosevelt

Hospital (now part of Mount Sinai St. Luke's). He gave me his best referral – the neurosurgeon who is now the vice chairman of the department of neurosurgery at St Luke's – and said he would not let just anyone mess with his back should he ever need help, and if he did he would go to this doctor without hesitation. He, like me, was aware of the potential complications and high rate of failure of spinal surgical interventions. I set up an appointment to see the neurosurgeon the following Friday morning.

It was a surreal experience driving over the George Washington Bridge at six in the morning to make the 7am appointment to see a stranger who could possibly help me or wind up crippling me if things did not go as planned. When I arrived, there was a young patient sitting in the waiting room in a wheelchair who had a cane and a back brace. A scheduling error had us both booked at the same time, and in my fear I deferred to let him go ahead of me. Half an hour later the doctor, George, wheeled him out and it was my turn. I politely thanked him for making time to see me so soon and gave him the laundry list of my fears and concerns. He listened without interrupting, nodding in agreement even when I went into my tirade against modern spinal surgery. He took my MRI disc, loaded it into a computer and began to exam me using the standard orthopedic and neurological tests I was all too familiar with.

After reading the MRI he showed me the location of the cyst and said he felt my pain was being caused by the pressure it was exerting on the spinal nerve roots, which correlated with my exact pain-level pattern. He suggested I consult an interventional orthopedist, and if that didn't work we could move ahead with a more aggressive surgical procedure to remove it.

The following Tuesday Judy drove me to New York City to undergo a procedure with an interventional orthopedist at the Spine and Pain Institute. I was so desperate I was now willing to let someone stick a needle into my spine to see if the cyst could be aspirated in order to avoid surgery.

The procedure unfortunately failed, and I left the institute quite despondent and in a lot of additional pain and discomfort. I remember Judy and me crying as she helped me walk to our car parked only two blocks away.

No easy way out for me was to be had. After another week I called George's office for a return visit. I was now seriously considering the surgery because to continue the way I was feeling and living was no longer an option. I had reached the end of my rope.

Once I committed to the hemilaminectomy that George recommended, I stopped all other therapies and tried to focus on the upcoming surgery. Prior to agreeing to have the surgery, my mental mantra, or repeated self-talk, was not positive regarding surgery. It went something like this: *They are going to kill me. I will have a heart attack or stroke from anesthesia effects. I will come out worse off or no better than before I went in. I will be a cripple.*

I knew enough about the mind-body connection to know that if I went into surgery with this mindset the self-fulfilling prophecy was sure to manifest, and that I had better change my tune – pronto! I was urged to call a friend for help – Sheri Rain, whom I had met the prior year at a healing conference in Mexico. She and her husband were members of a Unity church in northern California. They had gone to Mexico with fifteen people who were members of their church and who had all undergone remission of their cancers. She immediately responded and channeled the following affirmation to me: "I choose to see myself in the light of Spirit, strong and hopeful, connected to the essence of who I am, filled with love, courage, grace and ease. Support surrounds me offering encouragement, assistance and love. My medical team is exceptional, competent, compassionate and responsive to the Spirit of who I am. I am a beautiful expression of divine presence, taking some time to heal my body, mind and spirit. And so it is! Amen!"

I'm happy to say that this affirmation worked, and I got a better-than-expected outcome, being discharged within two hours of the three-hour surgery with no more radicular pain in my back or legs! Divine timing and protection were in operation for me. I am eternally grateful to Sheri for giving me this affirmation in my time of need.

It's been quite a learning experience having to face my fears and doing something I vowed *never* to do. I'm forever changed as a result of this experience. And I have a lot more respect and appreciation for modern medical technology and what it has to offer. Nothing else was able to afford me relief.

There is a time and place for *all* healing methods, and we are fortunate that in times of need the universe conspires to support us with people, resources and help in the most unexpected and unimaginable ways. I feel blessed to have had that kind of support throughout this entire journey.

MORE COINCIDENCES? YOU DECIDE!

You won't miss a sign from the universe. It will keep getting louder and louder until you get it.
—unknown

S everal years ago I attended a week-long training program for self-development at the Hoffman Institute. Just before the event I had completed reading a book entitled *The Monk Who Sold His Ferrari* by Robin Sharma, a self-motivation speaker. I arrived at the training site, registered and headed to the dining room for lunch.

The first person who sat beside me that day was a man named Robin. We were instructed at the registration table not to tell anyone at the seminar what we did for a living, where we lived or our last name. This would provide a sense of anonymity, and at graduation we would reveal those details. But when Robin told me his name, I immediately knew he was the author of the book I had just finished reading! I commented to him about that, and he just smiled.

At graduation a week later, Robin Sharma confirmed what I already knew. Shortly thereafter I attended a chiropractic seminar at which he was the featured guest speaker! I vividly remember his telling me that he had tried to become an author and still maintain his law practice, but it hadn't worked for him. He had to let his practice go to fully embrace becoming a full-time author and motivational speaker.

I am now in the same position myself, and I have decided to retire completely from active practice and pursue a career as a writer and public speaker. That was the message that I needed to hear! The universe was speaking to me through him.

After my dad passed away someone suggested I read a book written by a psychotherapist, Alexandra Kennedy, entitled *Losing a Parent: Passage to a New Way of Living*. I immediately bought the book but for some reason I was reluctant to read it right away. Six years later when my mom passed away, I found the book on my shelf and read it immediately. I found it very helpful, with lots of practical suggestions for anyone dealing with grief, especially the grief associated with losing a parent.

The day I completed reading the book I took a ride with Judy to Woodstock, New York, to attend the annual film festival there. While walking around trying to find a restaurant, I noticed a flyer in a store window announcing a workshop being offered by Alexandra Kennedy in nearby Kingston, New York. After trying to get into several restaurants in Woodstock without success because of the overflowing crowds attending the film festival, we decided to drive a half hour to Kingston after securing a reservation at a well-known restaurant.

Less than one minute after being seated, in walked Kennedy and she sat right next to us! I immediately recognized her from the photo on her book cover. I politely shared with her the story of how I had bought the book some six years ago but had only just finished reading it after losing my mom. She was very gracious and immediately invited Judy and me to attend the second part of her workshop after lunch as her guests. We happily accepted. Judy had recently lost her brother, so it was timely for us to attend as we were both dealing with the grief associated with losing a family member.

The universe had prearranged the meeting at just at the right time and place, and the workshop was just what we needed. Again, in real estate it's location, location, location; in life it's timing, timing, timing!

Some years ago while attending a continuing education seminar in Florida, I met a man at lunch whose wife was a vendor at the event. He revealed that he was a former TV broadcaster and was recently let go by the network and looking for a new career. He told me how former CBS reporter Roland Smith had been a spiritual mentor to him at his last network assignment.

The next week I went hiking at Lake Mohonk in New Paltz, New York, and while waiting to retrieve my car from the valet, I noticed none other than Roland Smith in line in front of me. I approached and introduced myself and recounted how I had just met a former colleague of his. We exchanged pleasantries and discussed our mutual love and appreciation of the Mohonk Mountain House and the Smiley family who founded it.

In the course of our conversation, I asked Mr. Smith where he lived and he told to me he had a summer home in the nearby town of Rifton. I had been going to Lake Mohonk for over forty years and had never heard of this town except that the night before I had attended a chanting group there! He told me he had been interested in joining a chanting circle. I asked him for his business card and when I checked it out I discovered that he lived just up the hill and around the bend from the location of the chanting group.

While vacationing at the Mohonk Mountain House, I decided to venture into the town of New Paltz to buy a book at the local book shop. I perused the self-development section and a book entitled *The Meta Human* by Paul Solomon caught my eye and attention. It biographized the lives of four pivotal human beings who helped change the world in some very significant ways. I bought it and went back to start reading on the swim dock. I discovered that one of the people discussed in the book was a gentleman named Dr. James Yen who was instrumental in the history of China for shortening the Chinese alphabet to only forty characters so the indigenous peoples could learn to read and write with less difficulty. He also introduced some new family farming methods that forever changed the way farming was practiced in China. Most of us in the West have never heard of him, but to the people of China he was a hero!

The only strange thing about this was that I knew about James Yen because my friend Keith Smiley of the Mohonk founding family had told me about him some weeks prior. On the way to the Mohonk dining room is a long hallway with pictures of famous people from former US presidents to environmentalists, religious leaders, etc. Dr. Yen's is there too.

While I was sitting on the dock reading, another regular Mohonk guest came and sat down by me. I casually remarked that I had just bought this book and in it was a story of someone whose picture was hanging on the hallway photo wall. He looked at me with surprise and remarked that Dr. Yen's two daughters and their families were "over there," sitting about twenty-five feet from me on the other side of the dock! They were there that day for a memorial service for their recently deceased father. I could not believe it and proceeded to go over and introduce myself and explain to them how I had just purchased this book about their father. They were unaware of the book but felt honored to hear how their father's contributions were recognized and honored in the book along with Mother Teresa's and others'. What were the chances of meeting them so easily, no less than on the day of their father's memorial service?

Fast-forward twenty-nine years...

I distinctly remembered Keith Smiley telling me how he had gotten to know and admire Dr. James Yen. Now, some twenty-nine years later, while telling Sandra Smiley, Keith's daughter, about my book, I mentioned two synchronistic events I had experienced at Mohonk, one of them the Dr. Yen synchronicity story. She asked me if I still had the book *The Meta Human*. I asked her why. She said that another Smiley family member, Gerow Smiley, who was now living full time in Redlands, California, had just contacted her wanting to know more about Dr. Yen. Gerow was tutoring a young Chinese student in English and for some reason the student was interested in learning more about Dr. Yen's work.

I told Sandra that when I returned home to New Jersey I would look for the book and keep her posted. To my total surprise and amazement, no sooner than fifteen minutes later we ran into Dr. Yen's only surviving daughter, Alice Yen-Hing, and her husband, Robert, who were just checking in at the mountain house along with thirty-two other family members for another family reunion! I immediately recounted the story of first meeting them some twenty-nine years earlier back in 1990!

What's the likelihood or chance that minutes before I was asked about Dr. Yen's history and work by a Smiley family member that another Smiley family member had just inquired about Dr. Yen? From my perspective they were slim to none. This is just another example of the one mind in operation, connecting the Smileys, me and the Yen family descendants. Right time and right place in action here. I'm thankful to Judy for recognizing Alice as Dr. Yen's daughter and pointing that fact out to me as we were walking by the registration desk at Mohonk. She observed them checking in for their stay and encouraged me to approach them with this synchronicity story.

EPILOGUE – IT CAN MAKE YOU WONDER

Learn how to see. Realize that everything connects to everything else.
—Leonardo da Vinci

We live in a universe of wonder, with stars, planets and galaxies all around us numbering into the hundreds of billions of star systems just like our own Milky Way galaxy. Ever since I was a little boy and spent many summer nights around a campfire I have been fascinated by the beauty and immensity of the nighttime sky. I remember at a very early age asking myself so many questions: How did all this come into being? Where did we come from and what is our purpose here on this seemingly small, insignificant planet we call Earth, the third rock from the central sun? Is there a purpose to our existence? Are we part of a divine plan or are we just a mathematical accident and the result of chance, probability and statistics? Did life here evolve from or out of the primordial sea as a result of lightening striking the ocean over many eons, forming the double helix we refer to as DNA? Are we just like flotsam and jetsam drifting with the will and whim of ocean currents, ultimately landing on hard land as backboned creatures?

Someone I once knew used the following analogy when discussing the mathematical model of the origin of existence: Imagine a random explosion taking place inside a printing shop and as a result of that explosion the complete unabridged dictionary came into being! Or better yet imagine someone standing with their back to a canvas and randomly throwing different-colored paints over their shoulder without looking at the canvas and lo and behold the *Mona Lisa* was the end result. Preposterous, you may say, but that's what modern-day scientists want us to embrace with their Big Bang theory on the emergence of our universe and the origins of life.

It is my contention and belief, albeit unprovable, that life here on planet Earth is not by chance and haphazard. I have had so many experiences – and I suspect you have had some or many as well – that demonstrate beyond any reasonable doubt that we are part of a plan or collective consciousness.

Carl Jung referred to this as the "collective unconscious" and maintained that synchronicity was evidence that we are all part of it – a type of worldwide spiritual web or internet, in modern-day parlance. Every story in this book is factual. Everything I have written happened to me over many years, in so many ways, and was in my opinion orchestrated by some invisible force. We don't have to call this force or energy *God*, for that results in only more arguments and disagreements as to the origin of the force. Suffice it to say "something" was responsible for working out all the details of the "chance" meetings and events as they unfolded.

I'm sure you have had some similar encounters in your life and have wondered, like me, how and why such events took place. They say that nothing has any meaning except the meaning you give it, so I leave it up to you to define or interpret the meaningfulness or lack of meaningfulness of such events in your life and the consequences that followed such "chance" encounters.

PERSONALITY TRAITS OF THOSE WHO TEND TO EXPERIENCE SYNCHRONICITIES

D r. Gary Schwartz published a book in 2017 called *Super Synchronicity: Where Science and Spirit Meet.* He's a professor of psychology, psychiatry, medicine, neurology, and surgery who directs the Laboratory for Advances in Consciousness and Health at the University of Arizona. He has written several books on this subject and is considered an international authority, and I feel fortunate that he contributed an endorsement for my book cover.

In his book Dr. Schwartz shared that his personal observation is that people who experience synchronicity on a regular basis share many of the following personality traits:

creative
open-minded
compassionate
caring
playful
curious
courageous
genuine
intelligent
discerning
mindful
intuitive
appreciative
successful
sane

7 – 6 – 5 – 4
HOW TO HAVE MORE
SYNCHRONICITY IN YOUR
LIFE

The universe is giving you signs every day: in your sleep, on your timeline, in your conversations, on the radio, in the sky – pay attention to the people you meet. The universe is communicating with you.
—*unknown*

D reams have a way of coming true and often help guide us on our desired life path, help answer a question or solve a problem, or are an answer to prayer. I suggest you pay attention to your dreams, for they are one of the ways Spirit uses to communicate with us.

B. J. Palmer, the developer of my profession, always slept with a pad and pencil next to him on his night table. He believed that the innate brain (the subconscious) communicates with the educated brain (the conscious brain) during the sleep state, and he would write down the message or messages he received so he wouldn't forget them the next day if he was awakened during the dream cycle. I, too, have experienced my innate brain trying to communicate something to my educated one, and often wake up in the middle of the night and jot down some message I have received from the deeper levels of my spiritual self.

Dr. Palmer referred to these messages as "thought flashes" and said they should not be ignored. During the sleep cycle our educated brain becomes quieter, affording our innate brain an opportunity to communicate with us. If one were to dive deep enough into the ocean, even during a hurricane, one would find the deeper water to be calm. One of my older patients was a World War II submariner and told me that during a typhoon they had to dive to extremely deep depths to find calm water or they would surely have been shipwrecked. As human beings, with our overactive, busy educated minds, we also need to dive deep during meditation to hear what Spirit or Innate may be attempting to tell us or we can miss the beauty of this way of living. When the noise of incessant thinking is quieted, we allow the innate messages to be heard.

I suggest you make time daily, preferably in the morning before you start your day, to check in with your essential self and *listen* to your internal guidance system. As my friend and songwriter/poet Bob Sima tells us in his song: "Meditation is the medication that helps to break the illusion of separation. We are one when we are together, and we are one when we are alone." We have forgotten this truth that we are *all* connected!

People often remark that they don't have time to meditate, and I always say to make time and schedule it as part of your routine and you'll find that the rest of your day will go a lot smoother and easier if you do!

If you find it difficult in the beginning to sit still and observe your thoughts, stick with it and over time it will become easier to settle down and listen to your *soul self*. For those of you who simply cannot sit, try a walking meditation. Find a path in the woods or near the water and take a walk, observing the natural world – no headphones please, and listen to what you are being guided to do or what your higher self is communicating. I do both nearly every day to check in before I get distracted by my self-active educated mind.

Below is the 7–6–5–4 formula to help you decipher your synchronicities:

Seven Types
Six Cosmic Reasons
Five Questions
Four Practices

Seven Types of Synchronicity

How and why do synchronicities happen and what do they mean? Here are seven different types with their causes to help you home-in further on your own events. Remember, these are just concepts:

1. **Precursor**
   Precursor synchronicities usually show up when we're having a troubling or distressing time in our life or maybe trying to make a major life decision that will affect our future.

2. **Deviation**
   In these synchronicities we might find ourselves suddenly changing directions and doing something improbable compared to our normal habits, feelings or circumstances.

3. **Expansion**
   These synchronicities usually happen when we go through times of significant spiritual growth

or transformation. They are usually linked to something symbolic like dreams.

4. **Message**

   These are related to "expansion synchronicities" and we usually experience them as signs or omens.

5. **Manifestation**

   These synchronicities are when something we see or hear is a direct physical manifestation of a thought or subconscious thought we had earlier.

6. **Artificial**

   These seem like synchronicities but are not, so be careful of that possibility and don't blindly trust every synchronicity.

7. **Opportunity**

   On the other side of "artificial synchronicities" are ones that come at the right time to help advance our destiny – our story, and feel serendipitous.

Like my stories, genuine synchronicities are all around us and have been happening throughout our entire lives. We all just need to wake up to the fact that our reality is much bigger than we believe! We live in a multidimensional universe and can tune in to other levels of reality beyond space and time.

Six Cosmic Reasons We Meet People

I believe everyone we meet along the path has been sent from beyond either to be a lesson or a blessing. Pay attention to the idea that someone has shown up in your life because you have been communicating with them on a cosmic or subconscious level. No one enters your life by chance.

Be prepared to learn a lesson or teach a lesson. If you have been feeling alone and lost, do not despair, for the universe will orchestrate the myriad of details behind the scenes and send someone into your life at just the right time and place. Know that divine timing is at work and you will meet them when you are both ready. Sometimes someone shows up and helps us make the correct decision or guides us onto the right path to follow. Some stay for a while and others are like ships passing in the night, touching us only briefly. Here are six possible reasons why we meet others along the way:

1. They are sent to remind us of something.
2. They are sent to encourage us.
3. They are sent to help us grow.
4. They are sent to awaken us.
5. They are sent to hold space for us.
6. They are sent to stay with us forever.

Five Questions

Here are questions to ask yourself after a synchronicity experience to help you figure out what just happened and the why – or possible meanings – behind the event:

1. Could what just happened be a precursor of something coming soon?
2. Did I just do something improbable that induced this?
3. Did I manifest this by dwelling on it earlier?
4. Is this a sign or omen from Spirit telling me what to do or what not to do moving forward?
5. Is this a serendipitous opportunity for me or has the universe placed this person or created this event as a guidepost to direct me on a certain path?

Four Practices

So many of my synchronicity experiences have taken place on beach walks or hiking trails as described in this collection of stories. Pay attention to what you are observing, for the answer is usually right there in front of you!

If you want to connect through synchronicity and experience more magic in your life, here are a few suggestions from mathematician David Hand:

1. Pay attention. Synchronicities happen to people who are mindful and notice things. When you go about your daily activities, keep your senses open to coincidental opportunities.

2. Talk to strangers. According to work by British statistician David Spiegelhalter, synchronicities often arise out of talking to someone you don't know.

3. Seek meaning. Whether you see a string of numbers on a license plate or hear a song on the radio, ask yourself if you can make meaning out of the experience.

4. Write it down. Keep a log of the synchronicities that occur in your daily life. The more you notice synchronicities, the more likely they are to happen to you.

FINAL THOUGHTS

- People move in and out of your life-path based on the law of attraction and the vibrational (energy) frequency you're expressing.
- Trust the organic unfolding of your journey.
- Your vibe will attract your tribe.
- You attract what you express.
- Life works like a boomerang. What you send out comes back – not always in ways you might expect.
- The universe is always speaking to you. *Pay attention!* It's sending little messages to get your attention and remind you that we are all connected and not walking through our lives alone.
- When you meet a fellow tribe member, you will recognize them by how you *feel* in their presence,

not necessarily by how they look.

- Everyone you meet in your life is either a student or a teacher at different times to you.
- No one is sent into your life by accident. They are either a lesson or a blessing.
- Trust the universe to send the right people into your life at the right times.
- What's meant to be yours is already finding its way to you, often through synchronicity!
- Focus on the powerful, euphoric, magical, beautiful and synchronistic parts of your life, and the universe will keep giving them to you!
- The universe will align you with people, things and situations that match the energy and frequency you are expressing!

The final thought I want to leave you with is:

At the end of your life, when you reflect back and connect the dots, you will come to finally realize that it was never random!

—Ken Harris

CONTACTS

What's Your Synchronicity Type and Story?

We all have the ability to connect to synchronicities every day; it starts by simply being curious. Does yours fit into one of the seven types? Did you arrive at answers by figuring out meanings? Did you apply all the ways to find more synchronicity in your life?

This is an invitation to connect and share your personal stories at info@doctorkenharris.com.

Contact Dr. Harris for seminars, workshops, keynote addresses and personal healing sessions at **www.DoctorKenHarris.com.**

References

www.attunement.org
www.DrWayneDyer.com
www.RamDass.org
www.JohnDenver.com
www.Mohonk.com

ACKNOWLEDGMENTS

They say it takes a village to raise a child, and I say it takes lots of people to help you write a book. First and foremost, a BIG shout out to my wife of fifty years, Judy, for listening over and over ad infinitum to my stories. She witnessed many of the synchronicities in this book and could repeat them verbatim if asked!

And another shout out to my parents, Louis and Catherine Harris, for the gift of life.

I would like to acknowledge the Spirit world and the Beings of Light who I believe prearranged many of the so-called chance encounters in my life journey. I have had and continue to experience so many God-incidences that literally defy mathematics and probability.

Make no mistake about it, the universe is intelligent and well-ordered, and what may at first appear to be random is in fact often divine order in action at the subconscious level of being. There is a field of consciousness that connects all of us at the quantum level, and when we live life with gratitude and appreciation for the gift of life itself, we then connect with the underlying field of infinite possibilities.

Thank you…

To my two editors, Donna Moore early on and Miriam Zernis for guiding me through the editing and reediting process back and forth with multiple changes in text and style of writing.

To Carrie Jareed, Project Manager at Capucia Publishing, and her team, for their expert advice and navigation through the book-publishing process. Her professionalism is outstanding!

To my fellow chiropractor, Dr. Bob DeBonis, for helping me some twenty-two years ago when I needed it most!

To Sheri Rain, who channeled a healing affirmation for me at a time of a serious health challenge. I am eternally grateful for her help.

To my Mankind Project new warrior brothers mastermind group for listening and encouraging me to finish writing this book – especially Vincent Falone, a friend of forty years.

To the people who endorsed this book and took the time to read the manuscript and offer comments and suggestions along the way.

To many of my former chiropractic patients who wholeheartedly let me share my stories with them while coming to me for wellness services.

This project has been a labor of love and I hope it will prove useful to anyone who gets the opportunity to read it.

CONNECT WITH DR. KEN HARRIS

Mailing Address:
Dr. Kenneth Harris
51 East Prospect Street
Waldwick, N.J. 07463

Phone:
973-506-8203

Email:
info@doctorkenharris.com

Website:
www.doctorkenharris.com

Facebook:
facebook.com/kenharrisdr

LinkedIn:
linkedin.com/in/drkenharris

Twitter:
twitter.com/drkenharris

Instagram:
instagram.com/drkenharris

ABOUT THE AUTHOR

Kenneth Harris, M.S., D.C., chiropractor, educator, lecturer, workshop presenter, author and keynote speaker, was the founder of the Waldwick Wellness Center in New Jersey. The center was a multidoctor facility providing all-natural health and wellness care for forty-five years.

A pioneer in holistic healing, Dr. Harris first established his practice in 1974 and in 1993 established the Mind-Body Wellness Education Center, dedicated to the exploration, understanding and promotion of the mind-body-spirit connection.

Dr. Harris is an honors graduate, magna cum laude, valedictorian and former professor of the New York Chiropractic College. He holds a BA in psychology and an MS in education.

Made in the USA
Middletown, DE
18 August 2023

36757511R00089